GW01314275

HORN ?

Horn Technique

BY

GUNTHER SCHULLER

LONDON

OXFORD UNIVERSITY PRESS

NEW YORK   TORONTO

Oxford University Press, Ely House, London W.1

GLASGOW NEW YORK TORONTO MELBOURNE WELLINGTON
CAPE TOWN IBADAN NAIROBI DAR ES SALAAM LUSAKA ADDIS ABABA
DELHI BOMBAY CALCUTTA MADRAS KARACHI LAHORE DACCA
KUALA LUMPUR SINGAPORE HONG KONG TOKYO

ISBN 0 19 318701 9

First published 1962
Fifth impression 1974

*Printed in Great Britain
by Compton Printing Ltd.
Aylesbury*

TO THE MEMORY OF

DENNIS BRAIN

WHO MADE THE WORLD A

BETTER PLACE FOR

MUSIC-LOVERS

AND

HORNPLAYERS

PREFACE

Much has been written about the beauty of the horn, and it has been praised, during most of its three-hundred-year history as an orchestral instrument, for its wide range of tonal colours and its ability to express everything from romantic yearning to heroic declamations. In my own experience, I have been surprised at the number of laymen and ordinary concertgoers who are more fascinated by the horn than by almost any other wind instrument. Everybody seems to know that the horn is reputed to be a devilishly difficult instrument; and even the layman, upon hearing some out-of-place 'blurp' or 'cracked' note, knows to look first at the horn section to find the culprit.

It is perhaps natural that an instrument capable of such an enormous tonal and expressive range should also be enormously difficult. As in all things in life, there is a direct proportion between a given result and the efforts necessary to obtain that result. There are unfortunately few *honest* situations, in this world of ours, in which a minimum of effort produces a maximum result. But then there is also a direct proportion between effort and effort's rewards. And the rewards for both listener and player that result from mastering the horn are indeed rich and satisfying. If, in throwing some light on the technical and musical problems of playing the horn, this book will help some aspiring student to attain mastery of his chosen instrument, my own efforts will be more than rewarded.

However, since—at a certain level—techniques must ultimately serve the music and its expression, and since technique and musicianship are inseparable, this book will deal with technical problems not only in a purely technical sense, but in musical terms as well. I am fully aware of the highly personal and subjective quality of what constitutes musicianship. Nonetheless I feel that, stylistic and national differences notwithstanding, many basic and specific things relative to the performance of music in our western civilization can and indeed need to be said.

Among others who have helped in the preparation of this book, I am especially grateful to Alan Civil for his valuable advice and criticism of my typescript, and to E. Emschwiller for executing the diagrams.

New York, April 1961

I should perhaps explain the letter-notation used in this book, for the benefit of readers who may use a different system.

The C 3 octaves below middle C is written C^1.

The C 2 octaves below middle C is written C.

The C 1 octave below middle C is written c.

Middle C is written c^1.

The C 1 octave above middle C is written c^2.

In each case the style runs from C to B.

LIST OF CONTENTS

I

THE INSTRUMENT AND THE
MOUTHPIECE

The first problem the prospective horn player faces is the purchase of an instrument and a mouthpiece. Since in many cases this first instrument and mouthpiece have a great influence on the initial formative stages of the player's development, considerable care should be exercised in this matter. The choice of an instrument is, of course, a personal matter, but certain fundamental minimum requirements can be set down to help the beginner.

If the player is an absolute beginner, he is well advised to seek professional advice from an established teacher or player. If the player is already at a more advanced stage and is buying a new instrument, it is well to remember that new instruments react somewhat inflexibly when first played. The valve action is usually still tight and stiff; and the air, gliding through the uncoated length of tubing, produces a comparatively cold and glassy tone. Although it is not a particularly scientific procedure, I have found that pouring milk (or at least water) through the horn, gives the tubing a coating which approximates the condition of a horn which has been broken in.

Obviously the instrument should play with relative ease, and it should have as many true-centred notes as possible, especially in the upper part of the range. The instrument, if second-hand, should be checked to see if it is in good physical condition. Too many patches on the bell and the tubing are a sign to proceed with caution, since it generally means that the original metal has been worn through. Too many patches also change the sound spectrum of the instrument and detract from its purity and firmness of tone.[1] An instrument of advanced age should also be checked for the tightness of its valves (inside) and the tightness of the valve mechanism (outside).

One word about the upkeep of an instrument. Although many instrument manufacturers and repair men suggest the use of light lubricating oils for the inside of the valves, I have found this to be unnecessary and even risky, if the oil used is not of superior quality. The saliva moisture which gathers in the instrument is sufficient to keep the valves rotating smoothly, and I have had several bad experiences with so-called 'light' oils sold by instrument manufacturers, which 'gum up' if not cleaned out and changed every few days, thereby slowing up the valves.

On the other hand, the outside mechanism of the valves (this does not apply, naturally, to string action valves) should be oiled regularly with a slightly heavier and more binding oil. This will prevent the wearing out of the joints connecting the finger keys to the valves. Since these metal parts are moved hundreds of times a day during the course of a practice session, rehearsal, or performance, it is wise to keep them well lubricated.

The choice of a mouthpiece is a much more difficult and vital matter, and the young student is strongly urged to seek the advice at the earliest possible stage of the most competent professional available. In many years of teaching, I have often had to witness the frustrations of young players who originally started on a poor mouthpiece and whose embouchure developed certain unnatural aspects because of an unsuitable mouthpiece. In such cases the damage to the embouchure was acquired unwittingly and

---

[1] Recent acoustical experiments by Boegner, reprinted in Hermann Scherchen's *Gravesaner Blätter*, No. 15/16, have proven conclusively that tone production on a horn is strongly influenced by the instrument's weight and the density of its metal. Too much weight affects the formation of overtones negatively and, as we shall see in a later chapter, it is the amplitude and great number of overtones that give the horn its unusually rich timbre.

unnecessarily; and while such damage is not always permanent, it may take months of painstaking practice and readjusting to correct it.

The 'ideal' mouthpiece is something so closely connected with personal tastes and personal physical needs, that it is practically impossible to generalize. What may be ideal for one player may be impossible for another. A high horn-player will certainly have different mouthpiece requirements than a low horn player. If anything can be said at all in a general way, it is that a mouthpiece should be of moderate dimensions and, in a sense, should be a compromise, if it is to enable the player to render with authenticity the many styles required of the modern player, from the lightest Mozart to the heaviest Mahler and Strauss.

While many players and teachers approach the choice of a mouthpiece from a purely physical point of view, I would like to suggest that this is not enough if we are to consider the playing of the horn as a fine art, not merely as a means of making a living. Since we are dealing with *music*, the physical requirements of a mouthpiece must be balanced against certain *musical* requirements.

The average horn player aspires to playing eventually in some first-rate orchestra; and it goes without saying that such orchestras play a broad literature encompassing roughly two centuries and an infinite variety of styles. A mouthpiece or a horn must give the player sufficient flexibility to cope with the demands of such a repertoire. For a mouthpiece or a horn that gives the player either too lean or too fat a tone will undoubtedly do injustice to some area of this repertoire. I think it is basically unmusical and a fallacy to pursue a specific tone *per se*, without considering the musical requirements to which end the tone should be only a means. In certain quarters in America and in certain countries in Europe, there are definite ideas on this subject which, while they may satisfy certain personal short-range viewpoints, in my opinion violate the fundamentals of artistic music-making. A large or a fat tone that remains inexorably the same is of very little musical value in a performance of a Debussy or Mozart piece, when that tone relentlessly penetrates the light-textured orchestral fabric. It is absolutely demonstrable that such playing, while perhaps satisfying to the player's ego, is diametrically opposed to the intentions of the composer. Similarly, an overly light transparent tone will not fulfil the tonal requirements of a Brahms or Mahler symphony. A truly artistic and imaginative player will not only learn to subjugate his 'tonal' personality to the style of the piece which he is performing, but will know how to vary the tonal properties of his playing even within a single composition, blending at times with the leaner sounds of a woodwind section, at others with the heavier sounds of the brass, and at still others with the mellower texture of strings. Moreover, a mouthpiece or a horn that limits the player to one type of sound is not only musically limiting but ultimately boring.

While these are artistic issues, I feel they must be mentioned early in the discussion, since very often the choice of mouthpiece (and horn) is so extreme that, after a short while, a more moderate middle course is no longer physically and psychologically possible. Early habits and training are notoriously tenacious. This is fine when the habits are good ones; it is dangerous when they are not.

In view of the above, the most sensible course, it would seem to me, is to find a mouthpiece which does nothing in extremes, but does almost everything relatively and equally well. Such a compromise is perhaps disappointing to the idealist, but it is the only practical solution. The idealist might do well to remember that the modern double horn is in itself an instrument based on an absolutely inseparable maze of compromises compared to the pure hand horn of, let us say, Mozart's day.

A mouthpiece has five areas which seriously affect the sound spectrum of the tone. They are the rim, the cup, the throat, the bore, and the backbore. The rim should be of moderate width and not too flat. Too wide and flat, the rim will provide the player with greater endurance, but will give him a dull tone, not too much sensitivity, and probably less accuracy in the high register. On the other hand, a rim

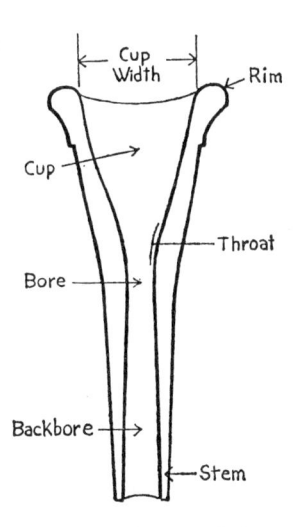

Fig. 1. *The Mouthpiece*

that is too narrow and curved will cut into the lips unduly, thus impairing endurance; however, it will at the same time increase embouchure selectivity by giving the player a better 'grip' on the mouthpiece. The inner edge of the rim should be neither too sharp nor too smoothly rounded off, the former characteristic especially impairing smooth slurs.

The depth and width of the cup affect the tone even more directly. A 'shallow' cup will produce a brighter sound and

B

make the high register easier; while the 'deep' cup tends to produce the opposite results.[1]

Large and small bore affect the tone similarly. The former makes for a fatter tuba-like sound that easily loses concentration, tonal purity, and therefore projection. A bore that is too small will produce a thin, penetrating, trumpet-like sound. Neither approach, obviously, gives us the mellow, round, ringing tone which, it seems to me, is the uniquely special quality of the horn.

The reader will have noticed by now that the advantages of a particular approach automatically bring with them inherent disadvantages. It is for this reason that the middle-of-the-road compromise approach is the only practical one.

The only other advice I should like to add on the subject of mouthpieces is: *pick a good one and stay with it*. Anyone who has ever experimented with different mouthpieces knows that 1) after trying two or three different ones, it is difficult to retain definite *objective* opinions about any of them—indeed at times it becomes difficult to retain one's sanity; and 2) one generally comes back to the original instinctively chosen mouthpiece. The truth of the matter is that there is no mouthpiece that is going to solve all of one's problems. Only practise and perseverance can accomplish that.

The compromise position I have suggested regarding mouthpieces seems to me equally applicable to the type of instrument to be chosen. Except in special situations (e.g. the performance of works with especially high tessituras), I think the ideal instrument for today's normal playing conditions is the double horn in B flat and F. It satisfies more of the demands made by the orchestral and chamber music repertoires than either the single F or the single B flat horns. The double horn, being a compromise instrument, admittedly has a theoretical loss in quality compared to the single horn. But this factor is more than outweighed by the gains in accuracy and flexibility. Certainly most modern scores

[1] See Chapter II on the acoustical properties of mouthpieces.

are either very difficult or impossible on either of the single horns. The quality of the double horn, moreover, can be very beautiful indeed, as the artistry of many fine players, past and present, can attest. In the hands of the sensitive player, the theoretical 'break' in quality between the two sections of the double horn can easily be bridged. In most instances the F horn part of the instrument produces a better tone in the lower register, while the B flat part gives us greater ease and accuracy in the upper register. Moreover, the double horn offers a choice of fingerings in the two middle-range octaves, thus affording a choice not only in intonation but also in tone quality, a matter of considerable importance in certain contexts.

One final suggestion: avoid purchasing an instrument that is too heavy. As already noted in the footnote on p. 2, most overweight instruments produce a dull, lustreless tone, which may sound big to the player but which in actuality does not carry.

Most elementary books of horn studies include fingering charts to help the beginning student. In many years of teaching, however, I have noticed that many students fail to understand the reasons for a given fingering and, therefore, the essential structure of the instrument. In order better to understand fingering problems on the horn, it is necessary to examine the relationship between the so-called 'overtone series' (or natural notes) and the construction of the modern double horn.

The overtone series (Ex. 1) is based on the same principle by which harmonics are produced on, for example, a violin string. Shortening the string progressively by half its previous length produces a series of overtones or harmonics. As can

Ex. 1

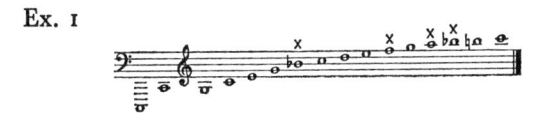

be seen in Ex. 1, the intervals of this ascending harmonic series decrease successively in size according to specific proportions determined by the vibrating wavelenghts.

On the horn, the pitch of its second natural note is determined by the length of the tubing. Or conversely, a vibrating wavelength that equals the length of the tubing will produce the second note in the series. On the F horn this note, sounding F, will have a wavelength of approximately 12′ 9″. This is also the theoretical length of the tubing.[1] The first or 'fundamental' note in the series (sounding F^1) has a wavelength of 25′ 6″, so that only half of this length can vibrate in a tube 12′ 9″ long. The third note in the series (sounding f), having a wavelength of 8′ 6″, accordingly fills the tubing one and a half times, while the fourth note (with 6′ $4\frac{1}{2}$″) twice; and so on, to the sixteenth natural note, whose wavelength will fit into the basic tube length *eight* times. Fig. 2 represents the harmonic series in table form.

In theory the harmonic series continues above the sixteenth note to the limits of audibility. However, since each successive wavelength is half the length of its predecessor, intervals between the tones thus produced gradually become so small (third and quarter tones at first, and later still smaller fractions), that they become indistinguishable to the human ear. Acousticians have calculated that between c^2 and c^7 (with a frequency of about 17,000 cycles, the estimated upper limit of hearing) there are 361 overtones. In that same range there are only 49 notes corresponding to our tempered chromatic scale.

The lower limit of the harmonic series on a French horn is determined by the fact that a pitch lower than the fundamental cannot vibrate in the available tubing. If only half

---

[1] For various compromise reasons having to do with the fact that the double horn consists in essence of a complex of *fourteen* horns (or fourteen different tube lengths), the basic length of tubing in practice is slightly less, and varies with different manufacturers.

No. of Series Note	Sounding Pitch	approximate Wavelength (in feet and inches)
1	F^1	$25' \, 6''$
2	F	$12' \, 9''$
3	c	$8' \, 6''$
4	f	$6' \, 4\frac{1}{2}''$
5	a	$4' \, 11\frac{1}{2}''$
6	c^1	$4' \, 3''$
7	$e\flat^1$	$3' \, 7\frac{1}{2}''$
8	f^1	$3' \, 2\frac{1}{4}''$
9	g^1	$2' \, 10''$
10	a^1	$2' \, 5\frac{3}{4}''$
11	b^1	$2' \, 3\frac{4}{5}''$
12	c^2	$2' \, 1\frac{1}{2}''$
13	d^2	$1' \, 11\frac{1}{2}''$
14	$e\flat^2$	$1' \, 9\frac{4}{5}''$
15	e^2	$1' \, 8\frac{2}{5}''$
16	f^2	$1' \, 7\frac{1}{8}''$

Fig. 2.

the wavelength of the fundamental fits into the basic tube length (see Fig. 2), it stands to reason that the next note below the fundamental will cancel itself out. This is because the pitch wavelengths in relation to the tube length decrease by half-lengths. Only half of the fundamental fits into the tube length, and if we subtract another half, the result will be zero $(\frac{1}{2} - \frac{1}{2} = 0)$. This acoustical phenomenon thus delimits the lower end of the harmonic series on the horn.

The diatonic system of Western music is largely based on the principle of the harmonic series. It is therefore not surprising to find that, by and large, the first sixteen tones of the overtone series correspond to pitches found in our diatonic scale. However, up to the sixteenth tone, four *impure* notes make their appearance (marked x in Ex. 1). The $e\flat^1$

(seventh tone) is quite flat, the eleventh tone is half-way between $b\natural^1$ and $b\flat^1$, the thirteenth tone half-way between $c\sharp^2$ and d^2, and the fourteenth tone a rather flat $e\flat^2$.

On the late eighteenth-century hand horn, if a player wanted to play in a key (i.e. harmonic series) other than that of the basic tubing of the instrument, he had to insert a crook into the tubing which increased the basic length. On the modern horn, the player accomplishes this same elongation of the tubing by pressing down a key, which turns a valve adding a certain length of tubing to the over-all length. Thus pressing down the second valve adds sufficient tubing to lower the pitch of the instrument by a half tone. It is, in other words, a fast way of putting the horn 'in E'. The first valve puts it 'in E♭', the third or first and second combined 'in D', etc. The greatest combined length of tubing is achieved by pressing down all three keys, thereby admitting six lengths of tubing, each adding a half tone to the instrument. In practice, however, due to the compromise construction of the double horn, both intonation and tone produced with all three valves is very poor. In fact, it is at all times advisable, for the sake of tonal purity, to use the minimum tubing necessary for a given pitch.[1]

On the F horn we have a complex of seven harmonic series, whose second natural notes are (see footnote on p. 8):

Ex. 2

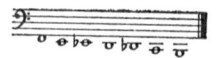

Each of these, of course, has its full set of sixteen or more

[1] In the last section of his ballet *The Firebird*, Stravinsky used a lip glissando in the harmonic series of B♮. In theory this was an ingenious idea, especially in 1909. But in practice the effect was miscalculated, because this particular harmonic series (all three valves on the F horn) is the weakest of all the ones available on the instrument. Its notes are colourless, weak, and difficult to control.

overtones based on the fundamental. On the Bb horn (or the Bb section of the double horn) we have another complex of seven harmonic series. These are a fourth higher than the F horn group:

Ex. 3

Even at a cursory glance, we can see that two of the series correspond: the first and second on the F horn, and the sixth and seventh on the Bb horn. Furthermore, if we visualize the natural note series above each of these pitches, we will discover that most pitches are represented in at least two series, and many others in three or four series. This means that they are available with as many fingerings.

For example, 𝄢 is the fourth note of the F series, the fifth note of the Db series, and the third note in the Bb series:

Ex. 4

In the middle and upper registers the number of alternate positions and fingerings is naturally increased, due to the increased intervallic density of the upper segments of harmonic series. g^1 for example can be produced in at least *seven* different positions. The following table illustrates this graphically (Fig. 3a).

Note in Series	Pitch of Series	Fingering	
9	F	0 (F)	⎫
10	E♭	1 (F)	⎬ Usable
8	G	1–2 or 3 (B♭)	⎭
7	A	2 (B♭)	⎫
11	D♭	2–3 (F)	⎬ Not usable (poor intonation and tone)
12	C	1–3 (F)	
9	F	1–3 (B♭)	⎭

Fig. 3a.

d² has an even greater theoretical choice of fingerings, although in practice most of them are too impure to be of much use (Fig. 3b).

Note in Series	Pitch of Series	Fingering	
10	B♭	0 (B♭)	⎫ Usable
12	G	1–2 or 3 (B♭)	⎭
16	D	1–2 or 3 (F)	⎫ Questionable (for special effects)
13*	F	0 (F)	⎭
13	F	1–3 (B♭)	⎫
14	E	2 (F)	
14	E	2 (B♭)	⎬ Not usable
17	D♭	2–3 (F)	
18	C	1–3 (F)	⎭

Fig. 3b.

*Used by Benjamin Britten in the Prologue and Epilogue of his *Serenade*.

A complete tabulation of note positions in the fourteen available harmonic series shows us a vast complex of alternative possibilities, which can be drawn upon by the wise player to simplify otherwise unmanageable fingering problems, as for instance in the case of certain valve trills. However, in all such cases the practicality of easier fingering patterns should be weighed against possible loss of tone quality and correct intonation.

II

TONE PRODUCTION

We have seen how the mouthpiece and the quality and type of instrument can affect the tone produced on a French horn. In this chapter I will discuss the remaining aspects of playing that affect tone production.

A. THE HAND POSITION

The manner in which the instrument is held is of the utmost importance. Tastes and national schools vary considerably in this. But in general, one can say that playing positions seem to be determined by the type of sound a particular school finds desirable. In the United States horn players tend to find a darker tone more useful, while in England a more open quality seems to be common practice. The English players no doubt find the American horn quality (especially some of the more extreme examples) muffled and too close to a tuba sound; while the Americans think of their English colleagues as lacking in the characteristic horn mellowness and too close in tone conception to the trombone or baritone. The French players have still another entirely different tonal concept, and no doubt find *both* the American and English approaches absurd. There are, of course, no absolutes in this kind of thing, and who is to say who is right. *Chàcun à son goût.* The various viewpoints on horn tone are held with a fierce devotion that one encounters otherwise only in religious controversies.

The position in which the horn is held reflects the above attitudes. The Americans, by and large, rest the bell of the horn on their lap, and in varying degrees turn the bell slightly *in* towards the body. The English players tend to hold the horn free of the body in a higher more horizontal position. Since neither approach can be proclaimed 'right'

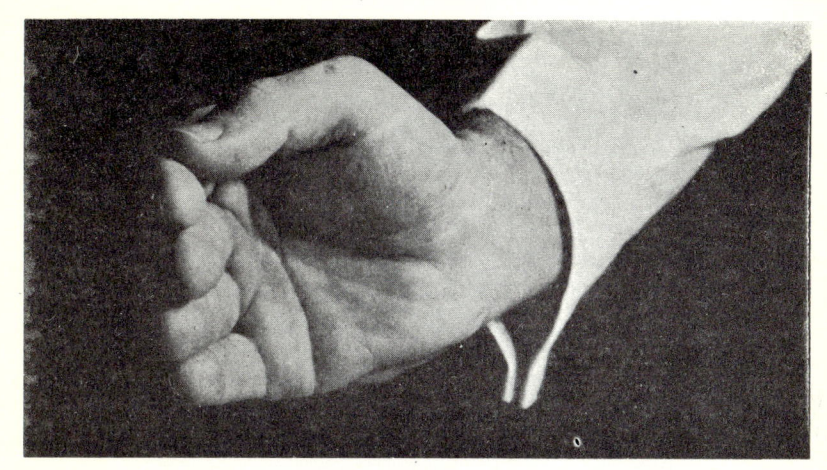

Fig. 4a. *Hand position*

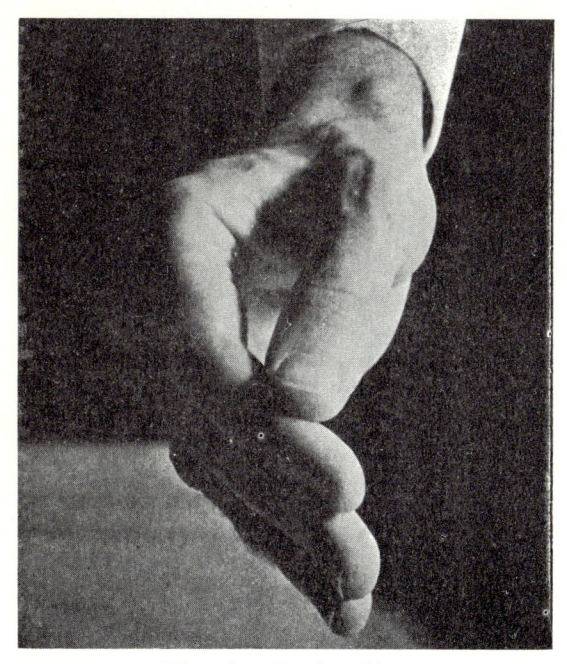

Fig. 4b. *Hand position*

in an absolute sense, the only conclusion, once again, should be that either position is admissible in so far as it permits the authentic recreation of a composer's intentions.

The position of the right hand in the bell of the horn has a significant effect on tone quality. Opinion is much divided on this issue, and each of the various approaches seems to have some points in its favour. My personal preference, however—again taking into consideration not personal *subjective* viewpoints, but demonstrable musical criteria—is for a hand position which helps to produce a velvety mellow sound, free and projecting in lower dynamics, which at the same time prevents excessive brassiness at high dynamic levels. Although breath control has an even more decisive effect on tone production, the role of the right hand should not be minimized. If breath control can be said to determine the basic inner nature, the core of a tone, the hand position can, like a garment, alter the external characteristics, the sheen of the tone.

The preferred hand position, which I refer to, can be described as follows: the hand is inserted into the bell *in a vertical position*, as far as it will go without forcing. The hand should be slightly cupped, and the fingers held together so that no air can pass between them, while the thumb should be in a relaxed position reaching towards the second joint of the index finger (Figs. 4a and 4b).

On this particular point I have found that a loose relaxed position of the thumb, not necessarily closing off the area between thumb and index finger, makes a better resting place for the bell of the horn. The bell thus 'sits' on the triangle shaped by the upper part of the index finger, the body of the hand, and the thumb as the hypotenuse. The hand, thus cupped, can give the proper support for holding the bell side of the horn, and at the same time—and this is what concerns us at the moment—direct the tone, the air column to be accurate, partially into the player's body near the waist. Naturally, if this is overdone, a stuffy tone will result. The player's ear or a teacher's advice can be the only arbiters. A little experimentation with this hand position will enable the player to find the desired tonal sheen.

In this connection, I would like to emphasize that the hand should be held in a vertical position. I find that in this way the hand has more control over tone and intonation, for the following reason: since the air column theoretically extends beyond the end of the bell—to what extent depends upon the frequency of the pitch—it stands to reason that the hand position I have advocated will form, with the body, a kind of channel through which the tone must pass, and upon which, therefore, the hand can have a direct effect. The tone is 'walled in', as it were, on two opposite sides

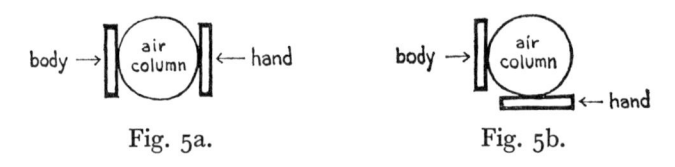

Fig. 5a.   Fig. 5b.

(see Fig. 5a). When the hand is placed, palm up, in a horizontal position in the lower part of the bell, as some players seem to prefer, it forms a right angle with the body. As can be seen in Fig. 5b, the hand, moving up and down, has no opposing 'wall' which can counter the effect of its movements. Instead of a wall, there is a non-resistant open space. The effect of the hand, therefore, is greatly minimized, and a harder quality is generally the result. Since the bell opening itself forms a perfect circle, the hand, in relation only to the bell, could be placed anywhere with *equal* effect. English players, holding the horn free of the body, therefore can (theoretically) place the hand anywhere in the bell with no variation in effect. If, however, the principle of reflecting the sound partially off the body is employed, it becomes obvious that the hand position in relation to the body is very critical.

The hand position described also allows for immediate hand muting and, above all, a maximum in hand flexibility to adjust intonation or tonal shadings.

While on the subject of the playing position, I would like to add that, regarding the left arm and hand, the player should once more find the most relaxed (but not *collapsed*) position. He should also learn from the very beginning of his studies to curve the fingers slightly over the keys (much as pianists are supposed to do), and by all means keep the fingertips in contact with the keys at all times. Good left hand habits will pay untold dividends later on in fast technical passages.

B. THE EMBOUCHURE

The position of the lips, or what is commonly called 'the embouchure', also plays an important role in the production of a fine tone. Technically the embouchure refers to the position and tension with which the lips and surrounding face muscles are held, in order that air blown through the lips may cause them to vibrate at certain speeds and thus produce certain pitches. Now there are four ways in which pitches can be altered by the embouchure: one is by pressure upon the lips from without (the mouthpiece and horn); the second is by changing the size and shape of the lip opening; the third is by altering the degree of tension in the lip muscles; and the fourth is the angle at which the air is directed into the mouthpiece. The first approach is controlled primarily through slight pressures applied by the left hand, while the latter three are governed by the movement of the jaw, the lower teeth, and the lip muscles themselves.

Before we investigate these points further, we had better find out exactly how the mouthpiece should be placed on or against the lips. Until recent decades, there were, I gather, two drastically opposed schools of thought on this subject.

These two methods were called by the German names of 'einsetzen' and 'ansetzen'. Both positions were, I think, valid at one time, when the division between high and low horn players was more acute. Today, however, when composers require a complete range from all but possibly the fourth horn player in an orchestra, the two extreme embouchure positions are no longer practical. New demands create new solutions, and the players have learned in recent generations to adapt themselves to newer conditions. And so we see that today's average embouchure is—once more— a compromise. It is neither 'einsetzen' nor 'ansetzen', but a workable combination of the two.

The most *natural* method for finding an embouchure that I know of is the following: relax the lips into an absolutely

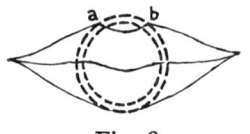

Fig. 6.

normal closed (not tightly closed) position. Take the mouthpiece and place the upper half of the rim on the upper lip, so that the rim catches the two slight curvatures (a and b) found in most lips (Fig. 6). This will put the uppermost curve of the rim into the 'white' flesh, and will guarantee that the mouthpiece is more or less well centred.[1] Now, *without* changing or lowering the lower lip position (i.e. relative to the upper lip), tense *both* lips into a slightly pursed position. In most cases this will put the lower curve of the rim *just within* the 'red' of the lower lip. Blowing air with sufficient

[1] Actually, in some sixteen years of teaching, I have noticed that very few embouchures are exactly centred. Slightly imperfect teeth formations seem to account for this in the majority of cases. The number of fine players who play with, in some cases, considerably off-centred embouchures are proof that the well centred mouthpiece position is *not* an absolute prerequisite, but I think it is generally desirable.

speed against and through the properly tensed lips into the horn will produce a pitch.

This procedure insures the proper representation in the embouchure of *both* lips, and at the same time places the upper and lower rims of the mouthpiece on the lips in such a way that pressure is exerted *on* the teeth just inside the gum line—assuming incidentally that the teeth are held apart at the proper distance of about a quarter of an inch.

Some players prefer an embouchure in which the rim of the mouthpiece sits *outside* the red of both lips. In this case the centres of both lips are entirely *inside* the mouthpiece. Although some players are able to use this embouchure effectively, I have had no experience with it personally. But from my experiences with students, I would say that such an embouchure is problematic and unsuccessful in a majority of cases. A number of students who learned to play that way and who, for one reason or another, did not want or were unable to change their embouchure, never developed either a beautiful tone or a good high register, and eventually gave up the horn. Some others were able to change to more or less the embouchure I have suggested, and have gone on to become fine players. But in general my experiences with that type of embouchure are not sufficient for me to discuss it in detail.

With the mouthpiece position I have suggested it is generally possible to negotiate with ease the entire four-octave range of the horn, and without a 'break'. This is accomplished, as I have indicated earlier, through the simultaneous interrelated application of four procedures: for *ascending* pitches, slight pressure is applied on the upper lip, the lip opening is made smaller by a proportionate inward and upward movement of the jaw and lower teeth (Fig. 7a), the lip muscles are proportionately tightened, and the air stream is directed increasingly downward and closer to the mouthpiece rim (Fig. 8a). For *descending* pitches, slight pressure is applied on the *lower* lip, the lip opening is made larger by a proportionate downward and outward movement of the jaw and lower teeth (Fig. 7b), the lip muscles are proportionately relaxed, and the air stream is directed more horizontally at a point in the mouthpiece cup closer to the bore (Fig. 8b). It can not be emphasized sufficiently that all these movements, especially those which involve pressure on the lips, must be moderate and *in proportion* to the interval change desired.

The halfway point between the two poles in embouchure positions occurs where the teeth are more or less vertically in line, i.e. flush (Fig. 7c), and where all the other movements and pressures are at an equally mean position. Since this position produces quite naturally a concert middle c^1 (or possibly a third below), I find it advisable for beginners to start with this note. Experience with beginning students has taught me that the f, a fifth below middle C, usually advocated as the first note for beginners, already represents a 'lower' embouchure position and is therefore not as easy to produce initially.

inward → Fig. 7a.   ← outward Fig. 7b.   Fig. 7c.

Teeth positions

The horizontal as well as inner muscle tension of the lips is controlled by the muscles in and around the corners of the mouth. It is a salient feature of the embouchure I have thus far described (or for that matter any embouchure) that the corners of the mouth must stay—no matter how relaxed or how tense—*in the same position*, i.e. the corners of the lips should not under any circumstances pull up or down. Special care must be taken not to 'spread' the corners (as in a smile) when going into the high register. The original corner position, which is halfway between that of a smile and a pucker, must be maintained throughout the entire range of the horn. If an analogy can be made, the lips and the mouth corners can be likened to a hammock swinging between two trees. The trees never move, while the hammock is free to pivot back and forth. If the corners pull away from the mouth centre, the lips will become too tight and thus will not vibrate properly. Imagine the trees suddenly leaning away from each other at a 45-deg. angle. Equally negative results occur when the corners relax too much and come forward. The resultant lack of tension leaves the lips in a collapsed state; or as if our trees were to lean toward each other, making the hammock sag. The best way I have found of teaching this correct corner muscle tension is to think of these muscles as coiled upon an imaginary axis and *anchored tightly against the teeth.*

I have mentioned that the direction in which the air stream is projected into the mouthpiece (Figs. 8a and 8b) is also of great importance. This aspect of tone production is seldom discussed or taught, and yet it is inseparable from the other three factors in producing a controlled tone on the horn. This idea is largely ignored because, in terms of

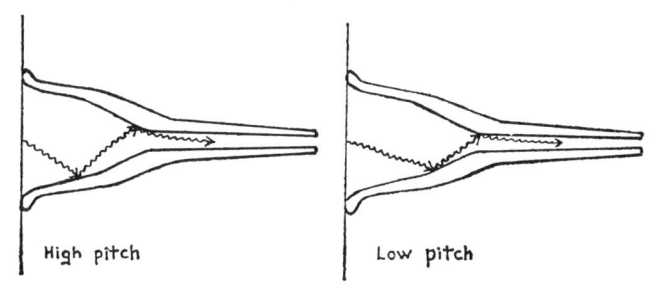

Fig 8a. Fig. 8b.

Direction of air stream

palpable physical movements, it is the subtlest of the four pitch-altering procedures. In fact, differences in the direction of the air stream can be *felt* only between larger intervals or extreme register changes.

This concept of 'air direction' is based on an acoustical principle of 'wave reflection', whereby the air stream is reflected or bounced off the walls of the mouthpiece before it enters the mouthpipe of the horn itself (Figs. 8a and 8b). For a high pitch (Fig. 8a), the air stream must be reflected at a point relatively close to the rim and lip aperture. For a lower pitch (Fig. 8b), a correspondingly lower reflection point is necessary. The necessity for the air stream to be directed in this way will be understood and felt most readily if the player will produce the natural notes (overtone series) in an unbroken slur. The actual shift of direction becomes quite noticeable, especially between the larger intervals in the lower part of the series. On the modern double horn, the availability of pitch-lowering valve action makes us less conscious of this directionality factor. Nevertheless, it is a fundamental aspect of the interrelated four-way process of tone and pitch production.

The direction of the air stream is controlled by the jaw and teeth positions I have described on pp. 19–20 (Figs. 7a, 7b and 7c). Obviously, a slightly forward position of the lower teeth will direct the air more horizontally, while a receding jaw position will point the air stream correspondingly lower. Such jaw movements also alter the angle of the mouthpiece in relation to the air stream. It is in this connection that I have found a slight 'riding up' on the upper lip for the extreme high register very helpful. It too helps to direct the air stream in a more vertical line, at a reflection point in the cup which is closer to the rim than to the bore.

The player should also guard against letting his cheeks puff or allowing air pockets to form behind either the upper or lower lips. I say this despite the fact that I have seen many superior jazz players (for example, Dizzy Gillespie) puff their cheeks to the point where I feared their cheek muscles would give way and burst like a balloon. However, there are more or less legitimate reasons for these deviations in the jazz field, having to do with special gifts, the extreme demands made upon these players, and the unique playing conditions (acoustics, dynamic levels, etc.) under which they work, which a non-jazz musician is not likely to encounter.

I am also an advocate of the moist embouchure. Although at a beginner's stage this makes the high register harder to attain, eventually, as the muscles strengthen and a niche for the rim is found on the lower lip, this feeling of insecurity disappears. It will then be found that a moist embouchure gives the player greatly increased flexibility, especially in slurring.

C. BREATH CONTROL

I have now brought the player up to the point where he is ready to attempt his first note. His mouthpiece placed correctly on the lips, which are pursed at the right degree of tension (controlled from the corners of the mouth), the player must now inhale through the momentarily relaxed corners. Immediately *after* the corners have returned to their tightened playing position,[1] the tongue moves quickly forward, producing the syllable 'tah' against the teeth (or lip, as the case may be; see p. 30). As the tongue pulls back, air is expelled through the lip opening, causing the lips and then the horn, which is nothing more than an extension of the lips, to vibrate.

Since a secure attack is one of the most difficult things to achieve on the horn, let me dwell for a moment on the inhaling and exhaling process which controls the success or failure of an attack. Inhaling should be done, especially at phrase beginnings, in a very relaxed yet lung-filling manner.

[1] I have had numerous pupils who at first reversed the sequence described here. They attack the notes *before* the embouchure has been re-tightened to the correct position—with less than satisfactory results.

The hasty, jerky breath tends to tighten neck, shoulder, and stomach muscles. A graph of the correct air-intake process would look something like this:

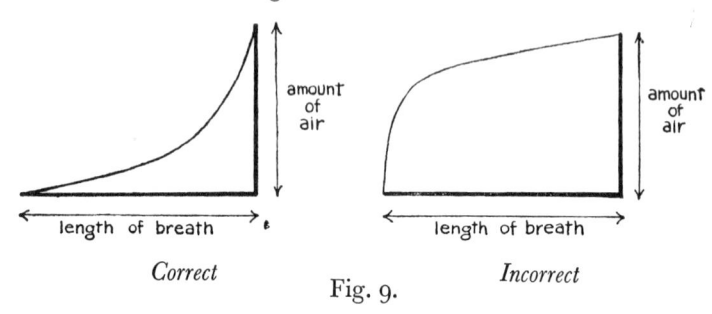

Correct   Fig. 9.   *Incorrect*

In general—and this is one of the most important factors in correct breathing—the taking in of air should always occur in time to the music being performed. This will insure relaxed inhaling, and will give to the breathing process a musicality specifically identified with the music being played.

Ex. 5   v=breath

(*a*) Mozart Horn Concerto No. 3 (1st movement)

(*b*) Brahms Symphony No. 2 (2nd movement)

(*c*) Rossini 'Barber of Seville' Overture

After a while, it gives the player an instinctive sense of timing in the several co-ordinated actions necessary prior to attacking a note, which will enable him almost to guarantee a note.

The end of the inhaling process should be as closely connected as possible to the beginning of the breathing *out* of air, as shown in Fig. 10. Both inhaling and exhaling should be thought of as a single uninterrupted act.

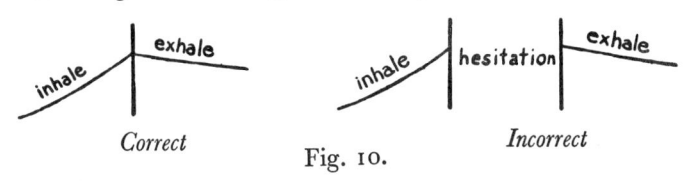

Correct   *Incorrect*

Fig. 10.

Hesitating between breathing in and expelling the air again serves no purpose other than to tighten various body muscles which should remain in a state of 'relaxed tension' for free natural playing. There is one exception, however. In the upper register, most players on an initial attack like to hesitate for the purpose of tightening the diaphragm into a strong supporting position. However, I wish to emphasize that this momentary hesitation is measured in fractions of a second, and is not long enough to choke back the air stream, unnecessarily tightening the neck and shoulder muscles.

At this point I must digress for a while to speak about the role of the 'diaphragm' in breathing. This term is bandied about a great deal, but in general many teachers and players still do not properly understand the nature and function of the diaphragm.

The diaphragm is a muscle which is situated in a horizontal position directly above the waist, and is shaped somewhat like a shallow round tent. The 'dome' of this tent is flattened out when we inhale, thus allowing the lower lungs to fill with air. And like all muscles, the diaphragm muscle, once contracted or expanded, must return to its original position and natural degree of tension. It is this natural tendency of the diaphragm to contract, after having been expanded, that is the prime factor in achieving what we call 'breath control'. The diaphragm is the only muscle with which the release of air from the lungs can be controlled, since the diaphragm is the only major muscle touching the lower lungs. This is also why breathing by filling only the upper part of the lungs ('chest breathing') is dangerous in horn playing. There are no muscles in the chest which can exert pressure on the lungs with relaxed control. Therefore the air issues from the lungs in an *un*controlled haphazard manner.

In horn playing the process of inhaling and exhaling is actually a more or less intensified version of normal everyday breathing, which even the casual observer will note as a slight alternating in-and-out of the abdominal muscles. In horn playing these movements are larger and more intense. But beyond this intensification, it is well to remember that the basic procedure is *exactly* the same as in normal breathing.

In normal inhaling only the lower section of the lungs is filled. The diaphragm muscle (tangent to the lungs) and adjacent abdominal muscles are thus expanded. The natural contraction of these muscles applies gentle pressures on the lungs, thereby expelling the air. In horn playing, since large amounts of air are necessary, all these processes are magnified. 1) The entire lungs (not just the lower part) are filled with air. (However, at this point I must emphasize strongly that one of the prerequisites of correct breathing is that the lower part of the lungs is filled *first*. Otherwise 'chest breathing' will result. I have found that the suggestion to breath along the 'bottom' of the mouth helps students to fill the lower lungs first. Conversely, I have noticed that breathing along the roof of the mouth leads easily to 'chest breathing'.) 2) The diaphragm and abdominal muscles expand considerably more than in ordinary breathing, to the extent that one can feel expansion almost around the entire circle of the waist, including the back. (This is what has led to the popular misconception that the 'diaphragm' is a circular ring-like muscle around the waist.) 3) The entire process from the moment of inhaling to the expulsion of most of the air takes correspondingly longer than in ordinary breathing.

I would also like to point out that the intake of air required for horn playing is so considerable, that this inhaling does (and should) become audible—as when sucking in air. Often students feel that this is wrong and try to inhibit this audible intake of air. It stands to reason that if the lungs are to be filled, and if the inhaling process is to take only a short moment, the 'rush' of air through the lips will produce a sound. Students should therefore not shrink from this, and should rather cultivate reasonably audible inhaling. As I have said, in actual playing, if the breathing is musically timed and not too jerky, it will not disrupt musical phrasing unduly. The breath will become a *part* of the music.

We have now inhaled and are ready to expel the air into the mouthpiece and horn. As in normal exhaling, the abdominal and diaphragm muscles will return to their original state of relaxed tension. For purposes of horn playing, however, an extra degree of control must be imposed. Different phrases will require different ways of expelling the air, in large to small amounts and at slow to fast speeds. We can now really appreciate the importance of the diaphragm and abdominal muscles, since *they alone* can control pressure on the lungs and, therefore, the amount and speed with which air is expelled. These muscles act as a kind of bellows. The return of the muscles to their normal positions can, in other words, be delayed or accelerated, thus affecting in a parallel manner the flow of air into the horn through lips and mouthpiece. At first, these muscles will be found to be weak, too weak at any rate to exercise absolute control over the flow of air. But over a period of months, with practice and conscious application of these muscles, they will gain in strength and control.

So far I have discussed only one aspect of the breathing-out process. There is, however, another area which is part of the over-all process of producing and controlling a horn tone. That is the control exercised upon the air stream by the embouchure. If the diaphragm is the motor and driving power in this process, the embouchure can be said to act as a rudder or steering device (see Figs. 8a and 8b). It *directs* the air and controls the speed with which the air enters the mouthpiece. Both of these factors control the speed of vibration in the lips and the horn, and in turn the pitch and tone quality. If we think of the lungs as the source of air, the embouchure (and at a further stage the horn itself) represent not only the destination of the air but a wall of resistant and *controlling* pressure.

The principle involved is a very simple one: the flow of a steady unchanging stream of air fed by the source (the lungs) can be increased by closing the opening through which it issues (the embouchure), just as, in a stream, a sudden narrowing of the river bed will cause a relative acceleration in the flow of water.

As the lungs gradually empty, the stream of air thins out. To compensate for this loss of air, the diaphragm muscle has to increase its pressure on the lungs, so that the flow of air may be kept steady and undiminished. If it is not thus sustained, the tone will naturally decrease in volume and probably in pitch. This is why students (and even profes-sionals) find the ends of long phrases harder to control than the middle. The degree of pressure exerted by the diaphragm and embouchure is dictated by the ear, which is presumably listening to the sound as it is produced. The more sensitive the ear, the more demands it will place upon the diaphragm and embouchure.

The air stream, and in turn, the tone, are also controlled by another organ, the larynx, which functions as still another element in this four-way chain of pressure I am attempting to describe. The larynx (situated in the trachea) is used in horn playing almost to the degree that it is used in singing. And of all the points of control I have mentioned it is probably the most versatile. The larynx is a valve-like organ which at one extreme can shut off the air from the lungs completely, at another (when open) can let the air rush out entirely unrestrained, and can, of course, adopt all gradations between these two extremes. To illustrate its function briefly: in playing a loud sustained note the larynx must be wide open; on a very soft sustained note it must close sufficiently (again the ear is the final judge) to slow down the flow of air to the proper volume. The larynx's other important function is to end a note. This is achieved by closing this valve still further to the point where the air stream being allowed to pass is not sufficient to vibrate the lips and horn. This feeling can be easily practised by singing a sustained 'Ah' syllable and gradually choking the sound off with the larynx. Obviously, the degree of abruptness with which a note is to be stopped can be easily controlled through a parallel abruptness in the closing of the larynx.

All four points of control (diaphragm pressure, larynx pressure, embouchure pressure, and the unalterable resistance from the mouthpiece and the horn) function in a completely integrated inseparable manner, and only diligent and analytical practising will give the player the necessary control assuming that he is not—as some players indeed are—a 'natural' talent, to whom all these technical processes are already second nature.

D. THE ROLE OF THE TONGUE

It is a well-known fact that the tongue plays a most important part in starting a note, in the 'attack'. It is less well known that the *position* of the tongue can influence negatively or positively the actual quality of tone produced. The tongue during a note, i.e. after the attack, pulls back into a relatively relaxed suspended position, arched slightly towards the roof of the mouth. For a high note the tongue must be arched high in the mouth, while for a low note the tongue can lie more along the bottom of the mouth. Actually the tongue's position is directly related to the position of the jaw and lower teeth, since the base of the tongue is connected to the pharynx. It would therefore seem to be natural that, as the lower teeth and lip move up for a higher note, thus making the lip aperture smaller, the tongue would automatically follow correspondingly along. Yet I have had many a student who tried to produce high notes with the tongue straining towards the lower teeth, and vice versa. An idea of how much the tone and pitch are affected by the tongue position *during* a note can be gained by moving the tongue up and down during a long sustained tone.

The tongue's role in the attack of a note is somewhat controversial. I have encountered excellent players who believe that the tip of the tongue must never touch the teeth, but instead should hit the gums on the roof of the mouth. Others think of the tongue movement as a 'forward' motion; still others think of it as a 'snapping back' kind of movement. Strangely enough I have found that, given enough talent and/or hard practice, reasonably clean attacks can be attained with all these different methods.

I personally feel, however, that the approach described below is the most direct and easiest to control. As in the case of tone production, the relative height or level of the tongue is again very important. For high notes the tip of the tongue, which should be pointed (not wide or flat), should produce the syllable 'tah' on the teeth. The higher the note, the higher the contact point on the teeth. High notes like high f^2 (concert), in fact, are attacked at the edge of the teeth and the gum line. By the same token, for low notes the tongue, now a little less pointed, may reach out as far as the inner curve of the upper lip. Between the lowest and highest

notes the tongue will adopt correspondingly graded lower
or higher positions, as the case may be. As can be readily
seen in figure 11, the tongue position at the moment of

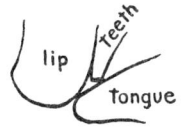

Fig. 11. *Tongue position (for a low note)*

attack is critical, since it controls the direction of the air
stream, a point already discussed on pp. 21–22.

As for the direction of the tongue movement, I believe in
a compromise of the 'forward' and 'backward' positions
alluded to above. This seems realistic since the tongue, for
any given attack, must move forward *and* back. The 'back'
faction claims that the release of air occurs only when the
tongue snaps back from the teeth or lip—which is true
enough. The 'forward motion' faction counters with the
equally true fact that the tongue could never snap *back* if it
had not first moved forward. They feel that this forward
movement actually controls the *nature* of the backward half
of the total operation. Basically I consider both movements
to be inseparable parts of one action. The player must learn
to control not one or the other movement, but *both* for a
perfect, relaxed, controlled attack.

In discussing which way the tongue should move, we
must divide the question into two parts: 1) In relation to an
initial attack (start of a phrase or an isolated note); 2) In
relation to attacked notes *within* a phrase. In respect to 1) I
am inclined slightly to the pulling away method, since it
gives you greater security in attacking a note. However, I
would caution against separating the forward and backward
movements too much for the following reason. Once the
tongue has reached the teeth or lip, it seals off the lip open-

ing and thus prevents the taking in of air. If the tongue moves into 'attack' position much before the beginning of the note, it automatically means that breathing will have to take place *before* that, which will in turn lead to the dangerous separation between breathing and playing against which I warned earlier (p. 25, Fig. 10).

As for the second part of the problem, I suggest the 'forward' approach, if not actually physically, at least *psychologically* as a point of view. For the 'backward' method unfortunately tends to lead to the very bad habit of stopping a note just previous to a new attack with the forward movement of the tongue. The notes thus produced might be characterized syllabically as 'daht', rather than 'dah' (see p. 30). This occurs all too often with beginning students, and must be immediately corrected. For if this habit persists, it leads to a kind of stop-and-go manner of phrasing, which prevents a sustained, singing style of playing. At high speeds, of course, the question of forward or backward tongueing becomes academic since the time allotted for both movements is measured in infinitesimal fractions of a second.

A subtle point often neglected in the study of attacks is that the air stream must follow *immediately* to sustain the tone. Even the slightest, physically almost imperceptible delay, will cause a 'poppy' attack, or one with a slight 'bubble' on it. The cleanest attacks will be those that have a *full* stream of air to back them up. This means that the air must be ready to go. As the water which is exerting pressure against a water tap is released when the spigot opens, so the air stream must be ready to flow immediately upon release of the seal between the tongue and teeth. The player should think of the tone graphically as shaped thus: ▬▬▬

not: ◄▬▬ or ◢▬▬ or ◥▬▬

or ►▬▬

III

WARM-UP AND OTHER
BASIC EXERCISES

I have brought the prospective student or player to the point where he is able to produce his first note. I have indicated how the note is to be started, held, and ended. This is the time then to introduce the subject of long note practice and, with that, the subject of warm-up exercises.

Wherever I have travelled there always seem to be a few players who feel—or at least claim to feel—that warming up is not necessary for them. Some of these are indeed excellent players, gifted with natural physical talent for the horn, to whom the warming up that a less natural player requires is anathema. Around such players a kind of myth arises that the warm-up is a waste of time, and only for weak players—that it is a 'sissy' approach to the horn. This gets so insidious at times that others, very impressed by the talent of these 'natural' players, feel inferior if they warm up, and consequently become ashamed of their cautious attitude—very often with disastrous results in their playing. For some reason the extrovert player who takes the horn out of the case and immediately 'runs' up and down the horn 'a million miles a minute', 'knocking off' a couple of high concert A's on the turns, followed by a 'fantastic' machine-gun-like cascade down to the lowest pedal F, makes a devastating impression on the naïve student or more introvert colleague. What the latter may not know is that a) our bravura 'preluding' artist has already warmed up a little in the privacy of his home, and b) that the rehearsal, performance or recording date may be of such a light inconsequential nature that the player—wise and experienced in these matters—knows that he will be able to manage without too much preparation. What the student may also not be aware of is that our 'no-warm-up-for-*me*' player may feel just a bit uncomfortable during the engagement, but, being talented and experienced, he is able to compensate for this sufficiently so that his playing does not suffer too obviously. But I doubt if even he would attempt the Beethoven Seventh or *Götterdämmerung* with a well-known conductor without warming up.

Of course, we all know the 'preluding artist', who sounds 'fantastic' *before* the concert and makes rather a mess of things *during* the concert. A word to the wise is sufficient. There is nothing ignoble about warming up, especially for the player who genuinely needs it, i.e. whose physical equipment for one reason or another is less 'natural' than it might be. The greatest artist on the French horn that I have been privileged to hear spent a full half-hour warming up each day. It simply took that long for his embouchure and breathing apparatus to reach the degree of utter sensitivity his great artistry demanded. That was Bruno Jaenicke, a German emigrant, who for some twenty-five years was the solo horn of the New York Philharmonic under such illustrious and demanding conductors as Mengelberg, Furtwängler, and Toscanini.

One other point about warm-ups. If the player's schedule calls for a heavy rehearsal in the morning, a free afternoon and a performance that night, he will do well to re-warm-up (on a reduced scale) before the evening concert. The original morning warm-up will not extend to the evening in such a case, especially after a strenuous morning rehearsal. During the afternoon the lip will tend to stiffen up, and therefore it must be loosened up and made flexible once more. I think anyone familiar with athletics will confirm the wisdom of this approach, and—as shocking as it may seem to some— there is something of the physically taxing 'athletic' nature to certain aspects of horn playing.

The following warm-up exercise (Ex. 6) is not only a warm-up, but a basic exercise with which to check up on the state of one's playing. It is also an excellent means of improving the fundamentals of playing (attacks, breathing, tone, etc.) if they have deteriorated. The exercise looks disarmingly simple, but is indeed quite difficult. If it is done perfectly, it actually guarantees that a number of basic playing prerequisites are in top form. (The remaining requirements are prepared in another exercise that will be discussed a little later on.)

I have been using this long-note exercise personally and in teaching for more than ten years. I am indebted for it to Mr. Richard Moore, first horn at the Metropolitan Opera House, my colleague for many years, who assembled this exercise from a variety of sources, including primarily the warm-up procedures of Bruno Jaenicke and Mr. Moore's teacher, Xavier Franzl.

Ex. 6

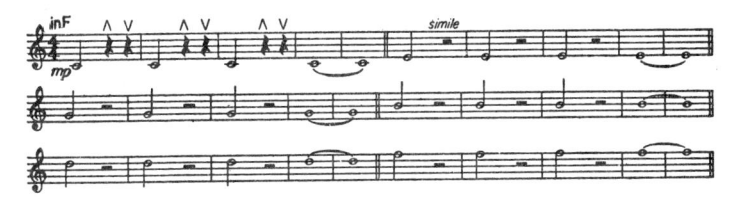

Continue four-note pattern on following pitches:

Any exercise, no matter how simple, can unfortunately be practised incorrectly. However, if the player will bear in mind all the points made in the previous chapter regarding tone production, this exercise cannot help but improve his

playing and give him a greater sense of security.[1] The
exercise should be performed at a comfortable dynamic
level, about *mp* (especially on upper register notes!). It is
essential to avoid any undue pressure on or forcing of the
lips—the idea of a warm-up being just that: to warm up
gradually. However, as I have tried to emphasize in the
previous chapter, it is most important that the tone be full
and round, steady (without twitching or quivering), and
absolutely even in dynamical level. It must be remembered,
that during any note longer than a second, the air supply
diminishes at a relatively fast rate. As this occurs, the player
must compensate proportionately in his breath support,
which in actual practice means that, for a note which is to
sound dynamically the same from beginning to end, the
player must actually perform *internally* (i.e. in terms of
breath support) a slight *crescendo* to counteract the diminishing supply of air. Without this crescendo the tone will
decrease dynamically.

The above exercise is also organized so as to provide
excellent opportunities for the practice of breathing. The
player must exhale completely on the third beat of the three
first bars, taking long deep breaths on the fourth beat. As
already mentioned (p. 24, Fig. 9), a sudden or hasty intake
of air is to be avoided. The breathing should take almost the
entire fourth beat, so as to connect almost immediately with
the attack of the note.

During the eight-beat note, the player must concentrate
on two things. He must avoid any movement or twitching
in the embouchure, and he must keep the air supply and the
various points of resistance in a perfectly sustained balance.
To the extent that deviations in these respects occur, to that
extent we can expect deviations in the tone. To find this

---

[1] It will be noticed that the exercise contains every pitch between
and (in F). It can, of course, be extended to include
notes beyond this range.

feeling of controlled 'relaxed tension' (or 'tensed relaxation') takes extremely concentrated practice, in which the ear assumes the role of critic.

After these long notes have been practised, the player—now partially warmed up—should turn to an equally simple set of exercises to limber up the muscles for playing more agile passages than sustained notes. For this I suggest the practice of scales and arpeggios in the following two-octave pattern, both tongued and slurred.

Ex. 7a

Ex. 7b

These scales and arpeggios are to be played in all keys. I strongly urge the player who is warming up to start with the lower scales and gradually work up into the higher register. After an especially heavy performance the day before, it is wise to start with scales as low as B♭, B♮ or C (concert). They require no undue pressure on the upper lip, and yet exercise and loosen up the corner muscles, which may be stiff from the previous day's exertions.

The tongued scales and arpeggios should be played with a bouncy lithe staccato. The attacks should be clean, and if the player follows through on each note with sufficient air, *no matter how short the note is*, he will insure the proper fullness (or centring) of the tone.

One of the problems in this exercise is to keep the dynamic level even throughout the two-octave range. Generally speaking, the upper and lower ranges of a given scale tend

D

to be weaker than the middle range. Here is another opportunity to compensate through breath support. If the player will give slightly more air support in these weaker areas (see Ex. 8), he can equalize the dynamic level.

Ex. 8

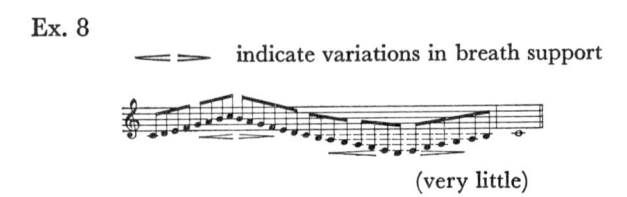

≖ ≖   indicate variations in breath support

(very little)

The foregoing applies to both tongued and slurred scales and arpeggios.

IV

LEGATO

A beautiful legato on the horn is one of its most precious characteristics. Since a large part of the horn literature consists of music where a good legato is required, the student is advised to spend much time on this problem.

The single most important factor in legato playing (slurring from one note to another) is our old friend 'breath support'. As we have learned, it is the air column that largely controls the vibration of the lips. Now the secret of good slurring is to keep this vibrating of the lips constant and controlled *between* slurred notes. Otherwise the beauty of the legato will be impaired or—worse yet—the player may find that the second note, to which he is attempting to slur, will not speak at all. It therefore stands to reason that extremely sensitive control of the air column is the key to a smooth, perfectly controlled legato.

The most common fault among students is that they generally give insufficient breath support in slurring. This is due primarily to the fact that there is in a proper legato a discrepancy between what one puts into the horn and what one gets out of it. That is to say, the internal approach to legato is seemingly out of proportion to the external result. It seems to be difficult for beginners and students (even many professionals) to reconcile these differences.

In order to get a smooth legato between two notes, in which both notes shall be equal dynamically and qualitatively, a *'breath crescendo' must be made* internally. This is especially true of any upward slur, and becomes more critical the larger the skip or the higher the register involved in the slur.

Now the secret of this 'breath crescendo' is in its timing. Let us call our two notes A and B. B must be prepared *during* A, to be exact during the last quarter or third of note A. If at this point a slight breath crescendo (controlled by the diaphragm) is made, the theoretical gap between A and B can be bridged in such a way as to make it inaudible. Incidentally, when I say 'breath crescendo', I do not mean a sudden huff of air *on* note B, but a smoothly accelerated increase of air *prior* to note B.

The principle I am advocating works somewhat like a canal and its chain of locks (see Fig. 12). As in a canal in

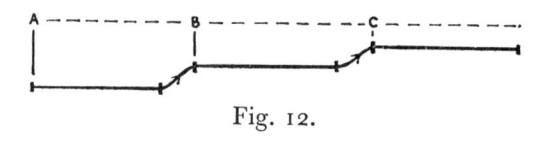

Fig. 12.

which the water floats a ship, the air carries or 'floats' the note. Before being able to reach the higher water level, the ship has to be lifted to that level. Similarly, before being able to attain a higher pitch level, the note has to be gently 'lifted' to that level. (In this 'lifting' process, the embouchure and valve action, if any is involved, also play an important role. I will discuss these points subsequently.) As the ship reaches the upper level, the lock is opened, and the ship is able to float out effortlessly into the main stream. Likewise, once the air pressure has been built up to give sufficient 'floating' support for the upper note, the tone will continue effortlessly at the new pitch level. The curious thing—and this is the point many students fail at first to comprehend—is that the breath crescendo, which is needed to lift pitch A to pitch B, gets *absorbed* in the lifting process, and does *not* show as an actual dynamic crescendo. Or if it does, it does so slightly that it adds to the musicality of the slur, especially if it is an upward slur. (Incidentally it is a fallacy to think that the above suggestions apply only to upward slurs. They do apply basically to downward slurs, the only difference being that the breath crescendo is a little more restrained. It feels more like constant rather than increased air support.)

As I have indicated, breath support is only one factor—albeit the most crucial one—in the production of a fine legato. The other two are the size of the embouchure opening, as controlled by the teeth, and the jaw and the timing and smooth operation of the fingers of the left hand.

I have described the function of the teeth in the closing and opening of the lip aperture in Chapter II. I can only add that in slurring, the teeth must move from one position to another—up or down depending on the direction of the slur—quickly and smoothly, 'clicking' into place almost like the gears on an automobile.

The fingering problems are less problematic, but are, precisely for that reason, often neglected. Many a slur has been missed solely through careless fingering. There are actually three aspects of fingering that are critical. One is the speed with which the key turns the valve, the other the impact with which the finger 'hits' the key, and finally the timing of this operation in relation to the movement of the teeth and the flow of air. Ideally speaking, the player's fingertips should never leave the fingering keys. Beginners would do well to watch this, as I have already warned. If, however, through habit patterns already established, the fingertips leave the key when in open (upward) position, care must at least be taken to return to the key, when next used, with a moderately gentle movement. This is necessary because the key puts the valve in rotation. If this turning of the valve is too abrupt, it will automatically have a jarring effect on the air column and impair the slur, which is so dependent upon a smooth uninterrupted flow of air. By the same token, the turning of the valve must occur quickly, though—I repeat—smoothly. The end of the turning process must coincide with both the end of the lower teeth movement and the fully increased flow of air.

Fig. 13 represents a diagram of the timing of this complicated threefold process (air, teeth, fingers). Notice that the starting points vary, while the 'finish line' coincides for all three operations.

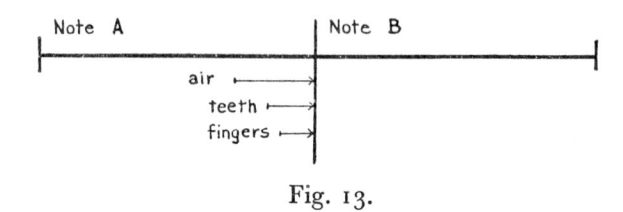

Fig. 13.

The different timing of these three operations, which should work smoothly *as a single unit*, can be achieved only through diligent and extremely self-critical practice.

Before I leave the subject of legato playing, I must speak of one other related problem—in my opinion one of the most widespread evils of horn playing. It is what I call the 'wah-wah' style of playing, in which each note is pushed and bent in a way that disrupts the easy musical flow of a legato or semi-legato passage. This style—to call it that is to flatter it with a euphemism—is not confined to one country. I have heard it in all countries where I have heard horn playing, although it seems to be less common in England.

Strangely enough, this manner of playing is seemingly accepted by all conductors, not to speak of lay audiences. Many a time I have been witness to a 'wah-wah' distorted performance of a phrase, and have heard the conductor praise the player. Never once did I hear a conductor tell such a player to phrase in a less distorted way. It is perhaps part of the past tradition of horn playing to allow standards of phrasing not condoned on other wind instruments. Conductors seem relieved when the horn player 'gets the notes', and generally do not quibble about matters of phrasing and intonation. I submit that, musical standards of horn playing having been raised to a new high by players like the Brains (father and son), Bruno Jaenicke, and Anton Horner (to name but a few), it is no longer necessary to accept a double musical standard for horn players. My guess is that most conductors fail to hear the difference, or at least are unable to cope with it on practical corrective terms.

I shall never forget hearing a famous player play the opening of the Sibelius Fifth Symphony in the following manner:

Ex. 9

When the even more famous conductor told me later that he could not imagine that passage played more beautifully, I was shocked, to say the least. The solo from the Tchaikovsky Fifth Symphony is perhaps the most maligned solo in this respect.

An analysis of the nature of the 'wah-wah' discloses that, whether tongued or slurred, the beginning of each note starts with a not quite centred tone and a correspondingly lower dynamic level. During the course of the note, both tone and dynamic level are expanded and heightened. Towards the end of the note, the original level is restored. At this low point, the connection is made to the next note. It is evident that there is a certain security—a feeling of taking no chances—in this 'sneaking-in' approach, and this indeed is the primary reason, I think, for the prevalence of this bad habit. It gives the player a chance to 'test' the note, to sort of *feel his way into the note* before playing it at full level. This is convenient, but most unmusical. There cannot be any musically sound reason for a series of seven notes (like the Sibelius) to sound in this 'egg-shaped' manner:

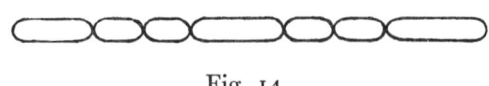

Fig. 14.

An idea of the degree of distortion involved can perhaps be gained by comparing the above diagram with the following, which represents the ideal of tone production, i.e. a

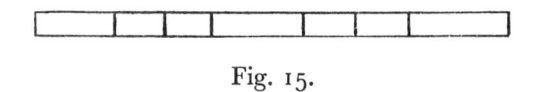

Fig. 15.

chain, not of sausage-like shapes, but of equally matched and fully sustained notes. This is, of course, much more difficult. I come back to my point about the internal versus the external crescendi. If a player is careful, the *internal* process need never show *externally*, at least not in any excessive fashion. For let us be clear about it: the wah-wah represents a lack of musical refinement, and indicates that in that particular respect the player is at a retarded stage. He has never worked out technically the final and musically most important stage of phrasing.

The most fundamental remedy for this malpractice is the exercise I have prescribed as a long-note warm-up. If practised correctly, the player will develop a healthy feeling for the pure shape of individual notes—a shape that is best characterized as a 'block of sound', i.e., a sound with a definite beginning (by which I do not mean an accented beginning), followed by the body of the note, no wider, no fatter and no denser than the beginning, and an equally full and definite ending. If, in addition, the wah-wah addicted player will for a time concentrate on approaching the beginning of each note—whether tongued or slurred—with a conscious effort at a direct *full* sound, he can in a short time eliminate this blight from his playing. Needless to say, proper breath support as outlined on pp. 39–40 is a prerequisite to musical phrasing. For without it, as should be clear by now, neither *complete control* of each tone nor graceful, seemingly effortless movement from one pitch to another is possible.

V

LEGATO TONGUING

In essence, tonguing is nothing more than a musical 'decoration' of a note. It should *not* be just a means of 'getting' the note. This is most important to remember if one aspires to any degree of sensitivity in phrasing. I feel that gradations in tonguing should be developed as early as possible, since limited tonguing abilities can quickly become a serious handicap, and make the proper performance of a great deal of the repertory well-nigh impossible.

A sharp attack will obviously be inappropriate in soft *dolce* passages. Conversely, a soft 'mushy' attack cannot possibly be musically adequate in a strong *marcato* phrase. I need not labour the point: the entire horn repertory contains phrases requiring not only these two extremes, but the complete gamut of infinite and subtle gradations between the two. Once this fact is fully realized, the necessity for complete tonguing control becomes obvious, and my original point becomes clearer: tonguing is a variable decoration of a note or a phrase, dependent entirely upon the *musical* context. If any doubt remains as to the validity of this theory, the player can easily convince himself, by placing the mouthpiece on the lip for any given pitch, and *without* using the tongue, blow air into the horn in increasing volume until the note starts vibrating. It is axiomatic that the amount of air necessary to start the note is a minimum amount. If the player can learn to guarantee this minimum air support, he can then be free to 'decorate' the beginning of a note with any degree or variety of attack possible.

A rather common weakness of students, as well as of occasional professionals, is that the attack is used to *get* the note, and, relying on this, the necessary air support is often lacking. While this deficiency may not cause actual 'crack-ing' of notes, especially if the player is able to provide the proper amount of air soon enough to 'catch hold' of the note, it will prevent the *immediate* focusing of the tone. Be-cause this impurity of tone production is slight, it is easily neglected by both student and teacher.

All these considerations apply very directly to what is called 'legato tonguing'. This is a way of tonguing used in countless solos (especially in nineteenth-century repertory) that is produced by articulating 'dah' or 'doo' instead of the 'tah' or 'too' of normal tonguing. It goes without saying that the degree of impact in the d's or t's is the controlling ele-ment in the relative hardness or softness of attack. It also follows that legato tonguing, written mostly by means of the following notation but employed even in many passages

Ex. 10

not thus marked, requires complete air support, since by itself the soft d of 'dah' will in all likelihood be insufficient to start the note vibrating. Therefore, in a passage consisting of two or more soft-tongued notes, it is essential that the air be *sustained exactly as in pure legato playing*. Since the consonant 'd' can only be produced by contact of the tip of the tongue against the teeth, it follows that this contact will momen-tarily interrupt the flow of air. It is necessary therefore—if the phrase is to have a sustained singing quality, i.e. without interruptions—to use the tongue discreetly and quickly. The tongue must move gently, flicking against the teeth in a motion that is, as I have insisted earlier, neither just forward nor backward, but an indivisible combination of both. In extreme cases of legato tonguing, the tongue only grazes the teeth. Here are some famous solo passages requiring legato tonguing.

Ex. 11

(a) Brahms Symphony No. 1 (2nd movement)

(b) Beethoven Symphony No. 6 (last movement)

STACCATO

If the attack of a note is in musical essence decoration, so is the ending of the note. This is unfortunately one of the most neglected areas, not only of horn playing but of all wind instrument playing. As we know from Chapter II, the closing of the larynx is the means by which we properly may stop a note. This can be done in various degrees of intensity and at various points in the duration of the note. When we stop the note almost immediately after starting it, we call this 'staccato' playing.

A common misconception exists that staccato playing requires a different technical approach than more sustained playing. Nothing could be further from the truth. Essentially, a staccato note is produced exactly like any other note; that is to say, a clean attack (in staccato fairly sharp and pointed) is followed by a fully centred tone and ended quickly by the action of the larynx. Common faults in staccato playing are: a) the attack, because of the speed with which the tongue is required to move, is often fuzzy and unfocused; b) the tone, because of its relative brevity, is neglected and allowed to sound thin and pinched; and c) the tongue, rather than the larynx, is used to stop the note. This latter fault gives the note an unpleasantly abrupt ending and makes the staccato sound choppy and aggressive. For my taste, the most attractive staccato is one in which each note is ever so slightly tapered at the end. This gives the staccato note a nice bouncy, fluffy feeling. Examples in which a bouncy staccato are musically necessary are the solo from Rossini's *Barber of Seville* Overture, already quoted in Chapter II, and Strauss's *Till Eulenspiegel* theme.

MISCELLANEOUS ASPECTS OF
HORN PLAYING

I have now considered all the fundamentals of horn play-ing, i.e. the absolute physical necessities for producing notes. There remain now a number of peripheral but none the less very important areas to be discussed, which will make the student or professional a better player.

A. INTONATION

The first of these is the problem of intonation. Naturally a prerequisite for good intonation is the acquiring of a critical ear. Given this, it is a relatively easy matter to play in tune on a horn—I would say easier than on most other wind instruments. For on the horn there are three aids in controlling intonation. The first is manipulation of the right hand in the bell. A slight opening of the hand—to be exact, a movement of the wrist *away* from that side of the bell closest to the player's body—results in raising the pitch. Closing in with the hand—i.e. *towards* the body side of the bell—will lower the pitch.

The second method of controlling the exact pitch of a note is through the embouchure opening. An infinitesimal opening or closing of the lip aperture which can be barely felt[1] will result in respectively lowering or raising the pitch. I have found that in practice a maximum of control can be achieved by adroitly combining both of the above methods, hand and lip, balancing one against the other.

A third possible means of controlling intonation is the choice of fingerings offered on the double horn, and even

[1] We have seen in Chapter II how the position of the lip opening plays a vital part in pitch control by determining the direction of the air stream.

on certain notes on single horns (see Chapter I, pp. 11–13). I would suggest this third approach, however, only as a last resort. I am against the indiscriminate switching of fingerings. I believe a player should learn one basic set of fingerings (with alternates only for special situations), and learn to live with these by means of the other two methods discussed directly above.

A word must be said regarding the tuning of the slides. Undoubtedly, this will vary with each instrument and each make of instrument. In principle, however, I would again suggest compromise tunings. It is of little value to get one note completely in tune, if that will in turn make another note (using the same slide) *out* of tune. The intonation of the second note may be so far off, that neither hand nor lip adjustments can bring it into focus. If on the other hand, a compromise tuning is adopted, *both* notes—it is true—will be out of tune, but not so much that they cannot be adjusted by the hand or lip.

For example, on most makes of horns, the concert g^1 is sharp with one fingering (B♮ horn: first and second) and flat with another (B♭ horn: third). The first fingering gives a slightly brighter sound, the second a darker quality. Many players prefer the brighter, sharper fingering on the assumption that it is easier to 'lip' a note down than up. I myself tend towards this position (although the quality of tone demanded in a particular context might on occasion cause me to deviate). Let us assume, then, that as a basic fingering a player has chosen to use first and second in combination. The first and second slides in their natural positions, i.e. all the way pushed in, would produce a g so sharp that it would be practically impossible to lip it down sufficiently. The player therefore must pull out one or both of these slides. He not only has to choose which slide, or whether possibly both, but also to what extent either or both are to be pulled out. He can, for instance, pull the first slide out quite far until it brings the g down to true pitch. That will, however, make all notes played only on the first valve (the entire A♭ harmonic series, for example) quite flat. Since on many horns the first slide is already a little too long (for other compromise reasons that most manufacturers endorse), pulling it out further will make all concert E flats and A flats quite unusably flat. At this point, in other words, we would have a presumably *in tune* G series and a very *out of tune* A flat series. A passage such as the following, Ex. 12,

Ex. 12

would present serious problems, since the G's would be in tune, whereas the E flats and A flats would be *very* flat.

The same argument could be presented against pulling out the second slide to bring the g down. In fact that solution is even more problematic, since the second slide is shorter than the first; it would therefore have to be pulled out still further. But even allowing for this, the above passage,

Ex. 13

amended to Ex. 13, would still have a similar disproportionate tuning.

I therefore suggest a compromise tuning of pulling the first slide out a little, just enough to bring the g within reach of *further* adjustment through the right hand and the lip. In practice, this means about $\frac{3}{8}''$ or $\frac{5}{16}.''$ While this will still flatten the E flats and A flats, it will do so only moderately. A *slight* opening of the hand easily brings these latter notes up to pitch, while a *slight* closing on the g will bring that note down. This approach has two further advantages. It allows you to play with the purest possible tone quality, it being an established fact that the more the total tubing of the horn is lengthened, the more impure the tone becomes. Secondly, this approach will adjust certain basic differences in tone quality between the notes I am discussing. Since the quality of first valve notes is *darker* in colour than most other notes on the horn, and since, as already stated, the first and second valves in combination produce a *bright* sound, raising and thereby *brightening* the former, and lowering and *darkening* the latter brings both sets of pitches *qualitatively* closer. This is particularly helpful in passages using both the G and A flat, as in this example from Strauss's *Ein Heldenleben*:

Ex. 14

or a G sharp going to an A as in Liszt's *Les Préludes*.

Ex. 15

Here the brightening and sharpening of the G sharp achieved by opening the hand (and closing the lip) brings the note qualitatively closer to its neighbours, A and F double-sharp, and simultaneously achieves the slightly higher G sharp tuning necessary in this context, because the G sharp is the major third of the chord of E and has a leading-note function in relation to the A.

Hundreds of such intricate intonational relationships exist on the horn, depending variously on the make and

E

exact intonational properties of the instrument, the position of the note in the harmonic series, and, above all, the harmonic context of the phrase itself.

In general, I have found that (on the Alexander horn especially) the best compromise tuning is obtained by pulling the first and third slides to the extent indicated above ($\frac{3}{8}''$ or $\frac{5}{16}''$). Since the F horn part of the horn is built fairly sharp, the F horn slide should be pulled out quite a bit, perhaps an inch or more. The B flat slide should be out only an eighth of an inch.

Two common misconceptions about horn tuning remain to be clarified. While it would seem theoretically correct that the F and B flat parts of the horn should match perfectly in intonation, *in practice* this does not work. Many players tune their horn by matching up the same pitch (concert f^1, for instance) on both horns. Actually it is advisable to tune the B♭ horn slightly higher. This will give an extra advantage in tuning the upper register high enough and will keep the sharp lower register relatively flatter.

The other error often made, especially by students, is to adjust the *main slide* in order to fix *a particular note*. If *one* note in a phrase is sharp it is silly to pull out the main slide, as this controls *all* the notes on the horn. Certainly it may tune one note, but will it not also flatten all the other notes in the phrase which were originally in tune? Despite the poor logic in such thinking, it is a widespread practice; and teachers should be on guard against it.

B. DOUBLE AND TRIPLE TONGUING

Some players are gifted with extremely fast-moving and agile tongue muscles. Others are more sluggish in this respect. I do believe there can be and are legitimate basic differences among players in this respect. In many cases no amount of practising will compensate completely for a 'slow tongue'. In fast tongued passages, many players therefore have to resort to what is known as 'double tonguing' and 'triple tonguing'. This is an ingenious method in which notes produced by means of the normal tongue movements of 'tah' and 'dah' alternate with notes produced by the syllable 'kah', thus giving us in combination 'tah-kah tah-kah' or, in triple tonguing 'tah-tah-kah' or 'tah-kah-tah'. When first practising this tonguing, the attack produced by 'kah' will be very rough. This is because in the syllable 'kah', there is no direct contact between the tongue and the teeth. (Obviously not, since the whole point is momentarily to skip the use of the tongue.) 'Kah', being produced towards the back of the mouth, can only indirectly—by remote control, as it were—affect the vibrating of the lips.[1]

This leads at first to rough attacks and to a lack of rhythmic control in the attacks. Initially, it is very difficult to produce the dual pattern of 'tah-kah' in absolutely even rhythm. The student can speed up the learning process by making the K of 'kah' very strong. He will thus be able to control the emission of air better, and get a quicker response in the vibration of the lips.

Achieving a clean, rhythmically controlled attack by the kah-induced thrust of air takes many hours of concentrated practice. It is absolutely essential that it be practised *slowly* at first. The student should not proceed to a faster tempo until he has completely mastered 'tah-kah' at a slower speed. Any cheating to accelerate matters has just the opposite effect. Although at first discouraging, clean attacks can eventually be attained. I have not known a single student who, once he had put in the necessary amount of practice, could not master double or triple tonguing.

C. THE LIP TRILL

A similarly difficult effect on the horn is the lip trill. Because it is not constantly demanded of the horn player, I

[1] This is another example supporting my point that the air, and not the tongue attack, is the primary force in starting a note (see p. 46).

recommend its study more as a means of obtaining lip flexibility than for the sake of developing the trill itself, although that will, of course, be very useful at times.

The lip trill is most often used on whole-tone trills. (Half-tone trills being impossible with just the lip, fingerings must be used.) There are certain parallels between the practice of lip trills and double-tonguing: lip trills must be attempted initially only at slow tempos, very gradually proceeding to faster speeds, until an actual trill is achieved. Again the important point to remember is to keep the two pitches rhythmically absolutely even. And, like double-tonguing, lip trills require untold hours—maybe months—of diligent practice.

The basic thing to realize about lip trills is that the two notes of any trill are not produced differently than in a slow slur. The process is exactly the same: a slight closing of the lip opening and an equally slight increase of air to obtain the upper note; the opposite to return to the initial lower note. The standard exercise for practising the lip trill consists of the following pattern:

Ex. 16

It is suggested that when the trill is first practised, the upper note be slightly breath-accented (as in the syllable 'hah'). This will facilitate accurate timing of the slur, and will assure a proper amount of air. Sufficient air support and the exact parcelling out of the air (neither too much nor too little) will in time enable the player to find the minimum effort needed to make the prime note of the trill 'break' smoothly into its upper neighbour. If conscientiously practised, the ease and speed of the trill will increase day by day, and eventually will lead to the mastery of this effect. I repeat, however, that it is primarily an excellent means of maintaining one's lip flexibility and steady breath control.

Another word of caution: there are no short cuts to learning the lip trill; any other methods of trilling (except for the use of valves, which *is* permissible in most orchestral situations) are musically not valid. The shaking of the horn or various 'gargling' methods produce unsatisfactory or ugly results.[1]

One aspect of trilling is often neglected. This is the problem of starting a trill fast and loud *immediately*. I therefore recommend that at a reasonably advanced stage of trill practising—and only then—the sudden abrupt trill be practised as well.

In cases of really recalcitrant trills, where, for example, the spacing of the two notes is particularly wide (as happens on certain notes on certain instruments), a compromise method can be adopted. This is to *think* of the semitone *between* the two notes of the trill (in trilling F and G, think F♯). With open fingerings for F and G, no F♯ will, of course, actually sound. By maintaining a basic F♯ lip position, very slight shifting to either side will produce the desired F and G, and will eliminate the necessity of 'travelling' back and forth the entire route. It is like sitting on the fulcrum of a see-saw.

D. MUTING

Muting can be done in two basically different ways: one with the right hand in the bell of the horn, and the other by means of a fibre, wood or metal mute, manufactured specifically for that purpose. Unfortunately there exists a great deal of confusion and just ordinary ignorance regarding ways of muting and *when* to apply them. The confusion

[1] There is an effect called the 'shake', so far primarily used in jazz. It is produced by shaking the horn, thus making the mouthpiece actually oscillate between two lip positions. This *externally* applied effect is not to be confused with the more *internally* conceived trill.

is not confined to non-horn players (like composers or conductors), but is widespread among players as well.

Many composers are not very clear about the difference in the sounds produced by using a mute and that of hand muting (or hand stopping). Not knowing the difference, they write in their scores simply 'muted' or the equivalent in their language. Often they write 'con sordino' when they really expect hand muting; and vice versa. Many players also assume that the composer and the conductor do not know the difference, and therefore do whatever comes easiest, which is usually to put a mute in the bell. A few composers, however, like Wagner, Mahler, Ravel, Debussy, Respighi, and Stravinsky, do insist on the differences between the two forms of muting.

Hand muting is designated either by an + or by the words *gestopft* (German), *bouché* (French) or *chiuso* (Italian). The use of the mute is indicated by the words *gedämpft* or *mit Dämpfer* (German), *avec sourdine* (French) or *con sordino* (Italian). When the above mentioned composers—all of them great orchestrators—differentiate between the two methods of muting, they do so because both approaches produce different tonal colours, as I shall show. It therefore behooves the player to follow the composer's directions in this respect, assuming the said player wants to perform a work as closely to the composer's intentions as possible.

Muting with a mute is, of course, a simple matter of placing a mute in the bell of the horn. It is not necessary to *jam* or *grind* the mute in. It is sufficient to place it in the bell, slightly touching the sides of the bell at a point where the width of the narrow end of the mute coincides with the width of the throat of the bell. In this way too, the mute can be quickly removed, which is often necessary. Also, slight intonation or quality changes can be effected immediately, even while playing. Whereas trying to move or remove a tightly screwed in mute while playing requires a twisting effort sufficient to upset the embouchure.

Hand stopping is an entirely different matter. It is a fairly difficult technique and, in addition, requires transposing a half tone. Beginners are often baffled by hand muting because of the transposition involved. In hand muting the hand closes the bell, preventing the air almost (but not quite) from coming out of the bell. Because of the size of the throat of an average French horn bell, the point at which the average human hand *almost* blocks the air column is fairly far in the bell. This causes—in theory and practice— a shortening of the tubing (the bell, of course, being a part of the tubing). This in turn causes the raising of the pitch by approximately a half step, and the player must therefore transpose down a half tone to compensate for this. To be more exact, he must finger a note a half tone lower than the one desired.

Considerable confusion arises from the fact that another distantly related form of stopping the horn, called 'half' or 'three-quarter muting', is achieved by a somewhat similar hand manipulation, and results in the *lowering* of the pitch.[1] I will return to this form of muting shortly.

It is important to remember that in 'hand stopping' the hand must try to close the bell as completely as possible. Beginners tend to leave open cracks between the fingers or fail to press the hand tightly against the sides of the bell. The feeling in the hand should be that of trying to 'spread' the hand in many directions. Special care must be taken to see that a) the thumb is not twisted in under the forefinger, and b) that the fingers and finger-nails are flush against the side of the bell. Once this hand position has been learned, a slight forcing of the air through diaphragm and embouchure pressure will result in the note 'jumping' into the upper pitch with the right nasal, piercing quality.

Because of the different lengths of tubing in the B flat and F parts of the double horn, the stopped hand position has

[1] Benjamin Britten has used this technique with great effectiveness in his *Serenade for Tenor, Horn, and Strings*.

different effects on the pitch. On the F horn it raises the pitch a half tone; on most of the B flat horn it raises the pitch fractionally more. For this reason, hand stopping must be done primarily on the F horn. I have found, however, that from concert b♭¹ on the B flat fingerings can be used.

As for half muting, it is a special effect, coming more and more into use with contemporary composers, especially in Italy through the influence of the player Domenico Cecca-rossi and the composer Luigi Nono. As the term implies, it is a means of half closing the bell, resulting in a half muted sound, with an *unforced* misty tone quality. It is a very unusual effect, giving the impression of a sound coming from a distance, a sort of echo effect. It can also be used for extreme pianissimo passages in very live acoustics.

In order to better understand the difference in approach and quality between the two forms of hand muting, I think it is constructive to analyse the *acoustical* principles funda-mental to both methods.

Before going into these differences, it is necessary to ex-plain the structure of sound spectra on the French horn. In Chapter I we became acquainted with the natural note series which is the fundamental principle basic to all conically tubed brass instruments. The unique physical properties of the horn, the unusual relationship between the width, shape, and length of its tubing cause the horn to differ tonally from all other instruments in that its tone is much richer in overtones than, for example, the human voice, a flute, or a violin. Fig. 16 represents an approxima-tion in comparative graphic terms of the properties of these four sound sources. From the diagram it will be seen that a single note produced on the horn is not a 'pure' tone (like that of a tuning fork or an electronically generated sine tone), but is a sound structure comprising *many* tones. One of these determines the pitch of the sound; the others deter-mine its timbre and tone colour. These accompanying tones are none other than our old friends, the overtones or

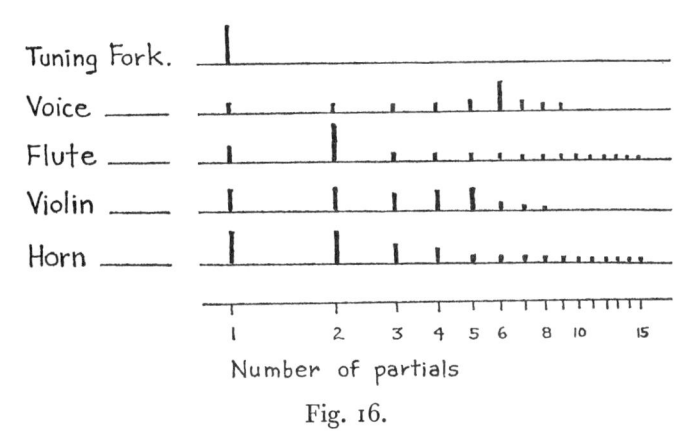

Fig. 16.

natural notes described in Chapter I. (In the context of spectral structures they are generally called partials or aliquots.)

It is a phenomenon of acoustics that the warmth and richness of a sound are in direct relationship to the number of accompanying partial tones. A greater number of such tones will create a warmer, darker, and richer sound. Conversely, a lesser number of partials will result in a brighter, thinner sound. The timbre of a sound is further determined by the number of low or high partials and to what degree of amplitude these occur. Acousticians have discovered that a horn note, in contrast to other instruments, contains *all* overtones. (In Fig. 16 only the audible or recordable ones are shown in the graph.) Furthermore, the lower partials are strongly represented, which explains the rich pungent tone colour of the French horn.

It is enlightening to study the spectra of the various notes in the natural note series. The diagram of Fig. 17 describes the spectral characteristics of the B flat overtone series. It shows us that the lowest note (contra B♭) contains the greatest number of partials, and that the number of partials decreases in the upper regions of the series. Thus the low B♮ contains twenty partials; the octave above fifteen; and the next octave only four.

Our diagram also shows us that in the first four notes of the series, the fundamental is weaker than the overtones. In contrast, the spectra of the fifth and eighth notes indicate that the fundamentals are the strongest of the partials represented. The greater incidence and amplitude of low partials in the lower range causes the relative warmth of tone in that register. Conversely, the greatly reduced number and strength of partials in the upper octave produces the comparatively brighter tone.

Here I must digress for a moment to explain the puzzling fact, that contrary to acoustical evidence thus far presented, the tone quality of the lowest natural note (B♭^{1}) is harder and thinner than that of higher pitches. This phenomenon is related to what acousticians call 'difference tones'.

A difference tone occurs when two partials are generated simultaneously by a played 'primary' pitch, and when the difference in frequencies between these two partials corresponds to the frequency of the primary pitch. To state it mathematically: the primary note (in our example B♭^{1}) with a frequency of 56 cycles, produces the accompanying partials of B♭ and f, with 112 and 168 frequencies respectively. The frequency difference between these partials, i.e. the difference between 168 and 112, gives us 56 cycles. The difference tone resulting from the simultaneous sounding of the two partials has a frequency of 56 cycles. This however, is the frequency of the played primary tone. Similarly, the frequency difference between any other adjacent partials always results in the number 56 (for example, the frequency of 168 cycles (f), subtracted from its next partner in the series, b♭ with a frequency of 224, equals 56, and so on up the series). As a result of this continuous frequential duplication of the primary note, the ear perceives *only* the primary note, i.e. without any partials, which as we have

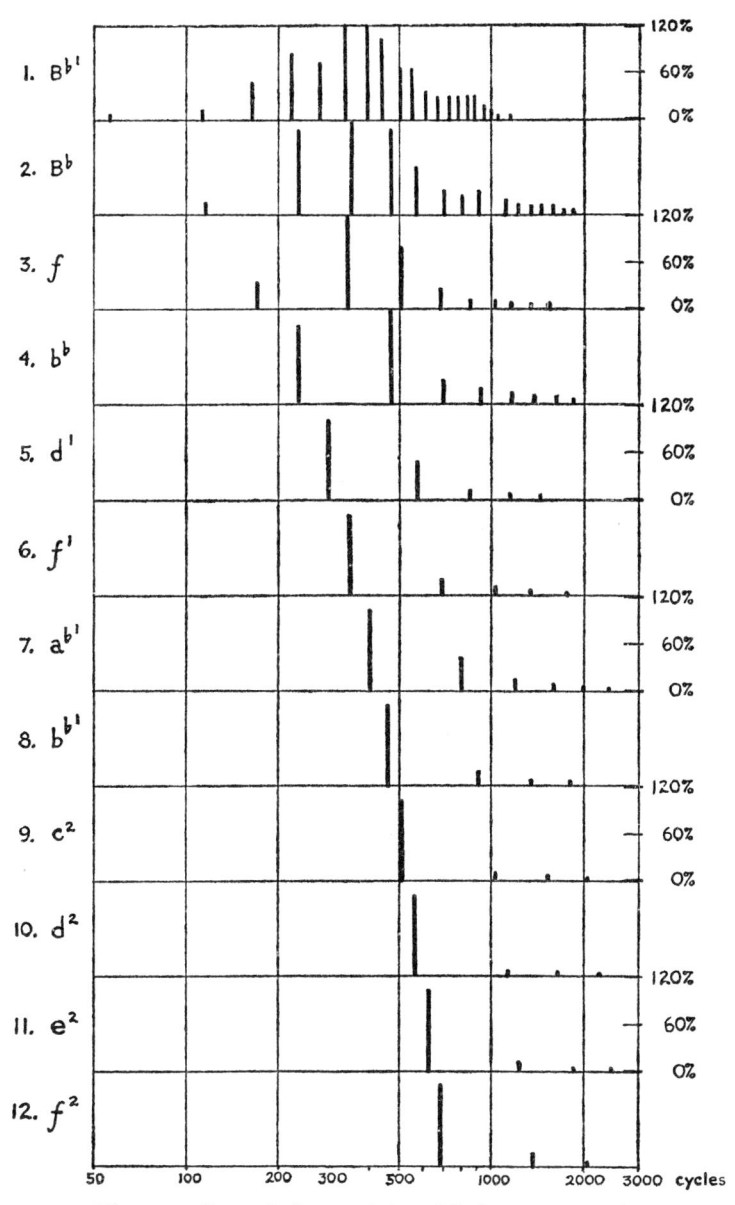

Fig. 17. *Spectral characteristics of B flat overtone series*

seen are in effect cancelled out. The tone produced thus is relatively thin and hard in timbre. All first tones in the series (pedal tones) have this same timbral characteristic. Low horn players compensate for this by using larger-bored instruments and mouthpieces.

In an earlier chapter I have already stressed the impact the hand position has upon tone quality. If we compare the sound produced with the hand in the bell in normal playing position with that produced by leaving the bell *completely* open, the latter timbre appears comparatively bright in quality and sharp in pitch. Technically speaking, it is a sound very rich in high overtones. The warming and darkening of tone quality, engendered by placing the hand in the bell, is the direct result of interfering with the development of *upper* partials.

A comparative analysis of the same pitch, played once *with*, another time *without* the hand in the bell, reveals quite different spectral characteristics. In Fig. 18a, note d^1 has two low partials, which are relatively well developed, and eight higher partials of much lesser amplitude. In Fig. 18b, the same pitch, now modified by a degree of hand colouration, has lost two partials, and the lowest two partials have increased in power, thereby giving the note a darker hue.

I have also pointed out in the chapter dealing with the position of the right hand, how the timbre of a note[1] is affected by even the slightest movements or position changes of the hand.

As we have seen, stopping is achieved by closing the bell as completely as the size and fleshiness of the hand will permit. If we play any middle-register note and, starting from a normal hand position, gradually close the bell completely, at the same time trying to hold the original pitch, we will see that the note will 1) invariably 'break over' into

[1] The intonation of a note is, of course, also affected by variations in the position of the hand, a subject discussed in greater detail in chapter VII.

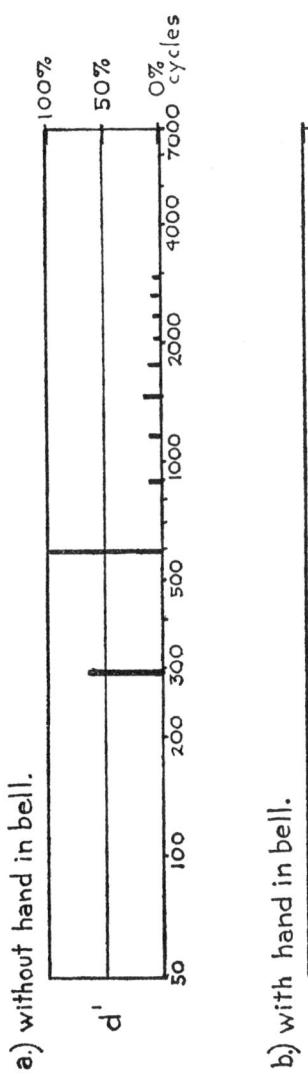

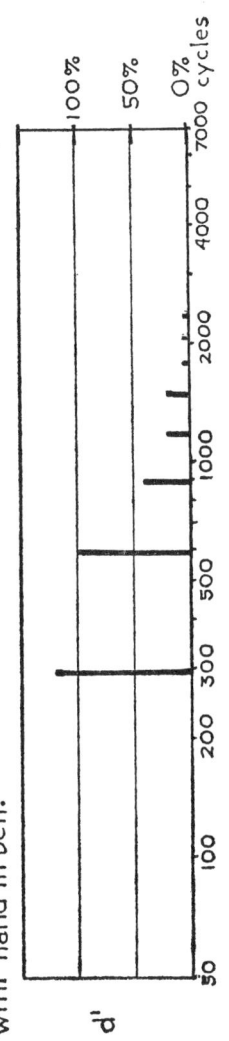

Fig. 18. *Spectral characteristics of* d^1

the minor second *above*, 2) become softer, and 3) lose in colour and brightness, acquiring a piercing, nasal quality. If we repeat the same process of gradually closing the bell, but this time also *relax* the embouchure slightly, we will hear the note change in the same three respects, except that the pitch will *flatten* by approximately a minor second. This is the effect known as 'half' or 'three-quarter' muting.

The acoustical explanation of these two experiments is that in full stopping the complete closing of the bell causes a *shortening* of the tube, while in 'half' muting, the tube is in effect narrowed and thereby *elongated*, thus raising the pitch in the first instance and lowering it in the second. As regards the changes of timbre, acousticians believe that in half muting the spherical spiral-like growth of the sound waves is impeded by the narrowing of the tube. To my knowledge no satisfactory explanation of timbre transformation caused by full stopping has as yet been given.

Returning now to the practical aspects of the two hand muting methods, it is important to realize that each approach results in a *new* overtone series: one a half tone higher, the other a half tone lower. We can demonstrate this easily by the following experiment.

First play the segment of the overtone series (the fourth to ninth notes) as indicated in Ex. 17a on the open F horn.

Ex. 17a

Now re-attack the first note, and while retaining the embouchure position *and tension* necessary for this g¹, close the bell with the right hand. The g will 'snap over' into a g♯. Keeping the new hand position, play the same F arpeggio as before. It will sound an f♯ arpeggio, i.e. the fourth to ninth note of an f♯ harmonic series (Ex. 17b). For the other half of the experiment, play the same open g once more. Then simultaneously close the bell *and relax* the embouchure until the

Ex. 17b

pitch has dropped to an f♯. From this new position the only arpeggio obtainable, which employs the fourth to ninth series notes, is the E arpeggio!

Ex. 17c

(In both methods, incidentally, the intonation of the lowest note may have to be adjusted somewhat.)

It is of some historical interest to realize that the method of half or partial stopping was the means by which players of the valve-less hand horn produced notes lying between the natural notes of the harmonic series.

Ex. 18

0 = *open.   The fractions indicate the degree of closure, which is approximate. Pitches other than those shown were rarely if ever used.*

I should like to suggest that the confusion among beginners regarding the two approaches to hand stopping arises from the simple fact that many of them experiment on their own and *by chance* find the 'half muting' method. Somewhere along the line, however, they have heard that muting is supposed to be done by transposing a semitone *lower*. If they happen to have experimented on the F part of the double horn producing a concert f^1, they would undoubtedly be further confused by the coincidence that, although the correct method of fingering that muted f^1 is the second valve, that second valve *unmuted* produces an e *or* an f♯ (!), i.e. both pitches directly above and below the concert f. The young player therefore finds himself playing an f, but he often doesn't know which way he got it: from above or below. If he turns to the average method books, he will find very little comfort, since most of them deal with the subject quite perfunctorily, and often fail to discuss half muting at all.

Many players, composers, and conductors are guilty of associating one single sound with all the various ways of muting. Nothing could be further from the truth. For the discriminating ear there are subtle but important differences, which sensitive players can use as imaginatively as a painter can work in shadings of one or two primary colours.

It is not easy to describe in words the difference in timbre between the three available methods of muting. However, in general one can say that 1) full stopping is most effective when used at strong dynamic levels to achieve a piercing, nasal sound; 2) half stopping is best used when attempting to evoke distant sounds, without much presence, downy and covered in quality; 3) using a metal or cardboard mute allows for the greatest diversity of muted colouring. In this latter approach, at high dynamic levels the sound can be quite brittle, sharp-edged and penetrating, although not quite as stinging as full hand stopping. At medium and low dynamic levels, the *con sordino* sound loses some of its edginess and can become quite veiled. However, it is my impression that the mute can never achieve the intimate, evocative quality of hand 'half-muting'.

If acoustical data are desired, analysis of the comparative spectra of hand-stopped and muted tones reveals that the main characteristic of notes produced by the first method appears to be the relative prominence of the fundamental or primary tone. In muting (with a mute), by contrast, a different sound spectrum is produced. The primary tone loses comparatively in prominence, and instead the upper partials appear in increased numbers, and (in high notes especially) in increased amplitude. This accounts for the rather penetrating timbre of muted notes in that range.

Except for muted high notes, the player should remember that the carrying power of the horn when muted is drastically curtailed. Therefore, unless a composer has already compensated for the automatic lack of projection, the player must compensate to maintain a balanced ensemble with other instruments. A passage marked *p* in an orchestral tutti should be played *mf*, at least, in order to be audible at all. In passages involving a more transparent texture, a *mp* would probably suffice. The player should also learn that the amount of dynamic compensating operates on a sliding scale from a maximum in the low register to a minimum for the highest notes of the range.

One final point on using a mute. The nature and construction of mutes cause the sound waves to be deflected partly into the cone of the mute and partly back into the instrument. This 'backing up' of the vibrating air column can have a disturbing effect upon the player's lips. It accounts for the difficulty players often find in attacking a muted note with a clear attack and unwavering tone. It is therefore often necessary, in attacking muted notes, to brace one's lips against the rebounding air column, as one would brace one's self in surf against an oncoming wave. Since the time that elapses between the initial attack and the return

F

of the deflected air column is measured in milliseconds, the tension in the embouchure must be firmly established *before* the attack. After the attack it is already too late.

E. VIBRATO

Thus far in this chapter, I have discussed aspects of horn playing that can be treated more or less objectively and on a fairly technical basis. When we come to the *vibrato*, however, we are entering the realm of personal taste and subjective opinion. Nevertheless, I feel the subject must be discussed, as certain purely *musical* and demonstrable points can be made in respect to vibrato. Beyond that, I can only say that the ideas I set down on this question have satisfied my own highly self-critical standards—self-critical from the point of view of the composer as well as the performer. They are offered not as binding dicta, but simply as suggestions— as a point of departure for other individual solutions.

I think one aspect of the vibrato on which most musicians (except in France) would agree is that it should be used with great discretion. Because of the basic intensity of a horn sound—compared to that of a flute, for instance, the degree of vibrato employed must be minimal; or else the sound will become quite unpleasantly overbearing.[1]

Vibratos are produced on the horn in a variety of ways, and I think they are all justifiable if used with taste and discretion. It really doesn't matter if the vibrato is produced in the throat, by the hand in the bell, or by gently shaking one's head or the horn. These (and possibly other methods not known to this writer) can be used to add a feeling of warmth and 'flow' to a phrase. I would like to emphasize,

[1] The situation in France is a complete enigma to me, not explicable in any logical *musical* way. There is no possible justification for the incessant superimposing of a vibrato, regardless of style or musical content. It is unmusical and insensitive, but worse than that, utterly boring in its lack of variety. Even third rate string players do not use the same vibrato *all* the time.

however, that vibrato is not a substitute for warmth and expression. These qualities have to be felt by the player, and no amount of vibrato can cover up a lack of genuine musical feeling, if that vibrato is superficially imposed.

Beyond this I would like to suggest that we retire the word *vibrato*. I think it is misleading as a concept. It implies that we *add* vibrations or a vibrating effect *to* the tone. It implies the *superimposing* of something *on* the tone. And indeed, it has been used by some players to cover up the lack of a good tone. I would like to think rather of an internal element *in* the tone that gives it motion. It should be something that makes the tone go *forward*, not *up and down*.

VIII

THE ART OF PRACTISING

A. THE ART OF PRACTISING

There are two primary elements that can make practising a success: intelligence and perseverance. What one student may accomplish through hours of hard, physically tiring work, another may attain in half the time by applying logic and intelligent thinking.

Many students never learn to think a problem through. Instead they stubbornly hammer out exercises which deal with the problem at hand only superficially or deal with an altogether different problem. While such practising is not completely useless, it is obvious that correct diagnosis of a problem will lead to more fruitful practising results.

On the other hand, some students analyse a problem quite correctly, find the proper exercises for it, but simply fail to put in the necessary time to alleviate the problem. Preceding chapters have shown that fine horn playing is the result of a vast complex of physical motions and nerve reactions. To co-ordinate and synchronize all of these into the smooth effortless operation that artistic playing demands takes time, for the simple reason that we learn through a combination of repetition and trial-and-error. More accurately, it is *a process of eliminating those physical movements that do not produce the desired result*, eventually reducing it to the one set of movements that *does* produce that result. Obviously this can only be achieved by sufficient repetition of a given exercise or study, combined with extremely self-critical analysis.

At this point we touch upon the player's will power, i.e. his psychological equipment, quite apart from his physical aptitude. Many a physically less-gifted player has overcome natural weaknesses by sheer hard work *and* will power; while many a naturally talented player has squandered his talent by lazy practising habits and a lack of sufficient self-criticism.

One thing is certain: nothing less than a *constant* demand for perfection will suffice to develop a truly artistic professional. To state it more concisely, given an adequate talent, a player will only be as good as he *wants* to be. The combination of physical aptitude, an intelligent analytical approach (positive, not negative, in outlook), *and* a zeal for perfection —these three ingredients rarely exist in one single person. When they do, he is apt to make a place for himself in the world of music.

While on the subject of practising, I should like to utter a word of warning to those who propose to take the horn seriously and to make it a career. If you wish to achieve a position prominent enough to assure you the kind of livelihood you think you deserve, *there must be some time in your student years during which you put in the six to twelve months of brutal hard work without which an enduring successful career is not possible.* This 'basic training' period is necessary not only in order to refine your playing to the highest professional level, but to build up the easily underestimated amount of resistance, both physical and mental, that the nervous tension of everyday professional playing demands. Any short cuts in this respect will sooner or later lead to trouble.

B. STUDY PIECES AND STUDY METHODS

It is important that the student practise study pieces which satisfy at least minimal musical demands and tackle a variety of specific technical problems. As obvious as this remark may seem, it is necessary to make it because there is altogether too much inferior study material on the market (especially in America at the high school level). Students who are serious about their horn playing should seek the advice of a good professional if they live in a locality which prevents their actually studying regularly with one.

There may be other study books as effective, but I doubt if any are superior to the old stand-bys for beginners: the Oscar Franz method, the two books of Kopprasch *Etudes*, and the Kling studies. They deal with the basic problems or horn playing in a disciplined manner. No more direct method of learning the fundamentals can be evolved than that contained in these various studies. They could perhaps be couched in different notes, melodies, or harmonic progressions, but the basic approach to anyone's problems is there, all spelled out in simple language.

When we look at the more advanced study material, I believe opinions can legitimately vary, depending upon the stylistic approach the player wants to develop. Certainly a great deal of French study material tends to develop technical agility and a lighter approach to horn playing, while some of the more advanced German or Czech methods underscore a more robust approach to tone production and register problems. I think at this point the player can only be advised to seek out the material which best suits his needs and problems.

My only quarrel with most of the basic study material (including the Franz, Kopprasch and Kling etudes) is that, for our era, it favours simple keys and conventional I–IV–V progressions far too much. Everything is in F, C, and B flat, and their related minors, apart from an occasional excursion into D flat. That is why I recommend very much using the six books of Maxime-Alphonse studies. For in these exercises all keys are thoroughly investigated, sometimes even within one study piece. This applies to the more elementary books as well. Not only is the student confronted with the countless fingering problems that can occur in the keys furthest removed from C, but he also learns to relate the visual image of these keys to their individual technical problems, a situation not encountered at all in the simpler tonalities. The Alphonse studies are also remarkable in their avoidance of horn study clichés. A favourite Alphonse device is to set up a pattern or sequence and then, just as the student is lulled into contented relaxation, the pattern is broken in very original and unconventional ways. This is excellent training for the student who expects to face today's contemporary music, which seldom contains reassuring patterns and sequences. These 'etudes' also provide a good test of the player's musical reflexes, and his ability to hear other than the most obvious pitch relationships. From the ear-training point of view alone, the Alphonse studies are highly recommended.

But even these excellent study pieces do not fully meet the ever-expanding demands of contemporary music—and by contemporary music I do not mean only works composed in the first decades of our century (most such works have already entered the 'standard' repertory), but the music of mid-twentieth century. Entirely new compositional and structural problems have led to an entirely new musical language, whose technical and stylistic problems need to be solved by the newly arriving generation of musicians. If we consider that almost none of the available study material prepares us even to cope with a work like the *Rite of Spring*, we must concede that this constitutes a sorry state of affairs. It is my hope that the study pieces published separately as a supplement to this book[1] will fulfil in some small way the urgent need for truly contemporary study material.

[1] *Study Pieces for Horn*, by Gunther Schuller (O.U.P.)

IX

SOME NOTES FOR
COMPOSERS AND CONDUCTORS

Being a composer as well as a horn player, I have often been asked advice by fellow composers about the feasibility of a given horn part. The horn seems to frighten most composers, especially as regards the extreme registers and such technical miscellanea as trills, the notational question of when to use the bass clef, and the like.

The two areas in which composers seem to err most consistently are muting and the use of the low register. I have discussed all aspects of muting in Chapter VII, and I urge any composer or conductor, into whose hands this little book should fall, to read that chapter very thoughtfully.

As for the low register on the horn, I find it is greatly overused by composers. The most characteristic range of the horn is that between concert a and d^2, and—if one knows how to use it—up to f^2. Below a the horn loses its true horn colour and its unusual carrying power.

The range between a and A is still usable, but the limitations just cited must be taken into consideration. (Below that the composer is advised to avoid using the horn altogether, except for sustained notes or special effects.) In the octave between a and A the horn becomes slightly unwieldy and colourless. Again, sustained passages make more sense than technically involved phrases. This is due to the very simple acoustical fact that a low note on a horn takes longer to 'speak' than a high note. c^1, for example, takes approximately 0.136 seconds to speak, while low Bb^1 takes 0.273 seconds, i.e. twice as long.[1]

Moreover, embouchure movements in the low register are larger than in the upper range and, therefore, take more

[1] These figures are quoted from Boegner in *Gravesaner Blätter*, No. 15/16.

time to accomplish. I have also previously pointed out that analysis of the spectra of lower pitches show us, if our ears do not, that the horn tone is warmer but at the same time duller than in the more brilliant and penetrating upper register.

As for the lack of projection in the low register, a composer could satisfy any doubts on that score by asking a horn player to record three pitches, one high, one medium and one low. Just by watching the VU meter of decibel ratings, he could quickly ascertain that the low note, even if the player attempted to produce it *ff*, would not 'kick' the needle as easily as a *mp* high note. A much more picturesque method of proof, one with which I have often amused myself, is to play these three pitches in terrain where an echo of one's playing can be heard. It will be seen that once again the upper register note returns clearly and with ease, while low notes have to be 'blasted' out of the horn in order to register at all, and then only very faintly. But perhaps the easiest proof is to listen to a horn quartet, as for example in Liszt's *Les Préludes* or the *Meistersinger* Third Act prelude. Here the composer can observe that, in *any* orchestra, he will have some difficulty in hearing the fourth horn, whereas the notes of the first or third horn (second highest) carry without effort.

Therefore, composers are advised to double lower register parts if they expect to hear them clearly; and conductors are asked to consider the fact that a low c simply cannot be made to project as strongly as c^2 two octaves higher. It is well to remember that all of these problems are more aggravated today with our highpowered brilliant orchestral ensembles. In Mozart's day, a second horn undoubtedly had much less trouble making himself heard in the smaller and more transparent ensemble. Today, too many composers and conductors take those earlier horn parts as criteria, and expect the low horn player to compete with trombones and trumpets whose bells—to compound the problem—face front, blowing directly at the conductor, while the poor horn player is blowing into somebody's pant leg or a set of kettledrums.

This brings us to the question of the bass clef. If horn parts are kept above these three notes, 𝄢 *it is never necessary to resort to the bass clef.* In the treble clef, in F horn, these notes look like this: 𝄞 which any horn player is quite used to reading, if only by virtue of the fact that the Franz and Kopprasch 'etudes,' which almost everybody studies, are filled with these notes written in the treble clef. The average player much prefers to read them that way, and does not have to waste precious rehearsal time asking which way the bass clef is notated, 'up or down'.

If notes below F are used, I personally prefer the so-called 'old method' of using the bass clef. Perhaps some day there will be a universally accepted standard bass clef notation. From every point of view, this is to be desired. But in this transitional period in which both methods are still in use, the composer can assure himself of an unequivocal bass clef notation by using the old method *in conjunction* with the above mentioned suggestion to use the treble clef down to F. If a player sees 𝄢 he will automatically know that the desired concert pitch is 𝄢 since no composer in his full senses would demand the only other possible reading 𝄢 . If he uses the modern notation 𝄢 and neglects to indicate which method he is using, there will always be a question on the player's part as to whether the note should sound 𝄢 or 𝄢 . An absolute safeguard, of course, is to mark clearly at the head of the part, which notation is used. That way no doubts can arise.

All that I said earlier about the low register applies even

more to *muted* low register horn writing. Muting cuts the carrying power of notes considerably, and if the low register is weak to begin with, it stands to reason that muted passages in this range will be inaudible except in the lightest instrumental textures. This note in a full orchestral tutti, though all may be playing *p*, will be simply inaudible, and the player might just as well leave the note out. It is doubtful whether his immediate neighbour in the orchestra or the player himself can hear it. If the player increases the dynamic to *f* or *mf* (which he is likely to do since there is nothing more frustrating than playing a note that is imperceptible to yourself), it may become audible, but acquire a sharp, edgy quality, that will in all likelihood be out of keeping with the given context.

What then is the answer? Until such time as other horns or mutes are devised, composers should avoid muting the lower octave and a half of the horn (i.e. below f), except if doubled, in very transparent ensemble textures, or for special effects. The bass clarinet, bassoon, muted trombone, or muted tuba are much more successful in this range.

The high register poses entirely different problems. Here the composer must consider *how* he approaches the notes between (sounding) c^2 and f^2. A good rule of thumb is to write at least one or two notes anywhere below c^2 into the passage, *preparatory* to the high note. It gives the player a chance to get a solid footing before negotiating the slippery environs of the uppermost range. It is also unwise to expect extreme high notes to be as strong as in the octave below. They simply aren't; a law of diminishing (dynamic) returns goes into effect above c^2. And composers who confuse these notes with a sort of fatter-sounding trumpet quality are in for some real disappointments. This applies also to the few available notes above f^2, which, in any case, should not be used at all, unless the composer is very sure of himself, or has checked the passage with a first-rate player. In most cases—even some notorious examples in past horn literature (Strauss's *Sinfonia Domestica*, Schumann's *Concerto for four Horns*, etc.)—the meagre result produced by these extreme high notes is not worth the monumental effort required of the player.

As for conductors, they are well advised to look the other way when a passage includes some delicately placed high notes. If the horn player 'muffs' the note, he is at least *as* sorry as the conductor: he has a lot more at stake. A look of surprise, disdain, or distemper on the conductor's part will do very little to alleviate the situation. High notes are always a treacherous matter, and if a man misses one occasionally, the conductor should not take it as a personal affront. This is all too often the case, because some conductors have the quaint notion that the modern double-horn player need only push down his thumb (B♭) valve, and out pop a series of perfect high notes. This actually happened to me quite a few years ago at the Metropolitan with a world-famous 'maestro'. A few minutes of thought about the position of those notes in the harmonic series (even on the B flat horn) would have revealed to this conductor how eminently silly his remark was.

Trills on the horn seem to be somewhat of a mystery to most composers. Here again, however, an easy rule can be followed. All half-tone trills are relatively easy and effective, since they must be fingered.[1] In almost all cases where difficult cross-fingerings are involved, the player with a minimum of ingenuity, can figure out alternate fingerings (especially on the double horn) to make the trill effective (see Chapter I, pp. 11–13).

Whole-tone trills, on the other hand, should be used with more restraint. Certain whole-tone trills are possible only as lip trills, and are therefore risky, since the lip trill is not

---

[1] There is no half-tone lip trill on the horn, except in the extreme high register; and those trills are not played that way since they can be fingered so much more easily.

an everyday requirement in horn playing. If whole-tone trills are to be used soloistically, a player should be consulted or the composer should be satisfied with the results, if they are less than desired. On the other hand, trills that are doubled or used in tutti passages are very effective, and can be managed in one way or another by most players. Good examples of this 'tutti' use of the trill occur at the end of Debussy's *La Mer*, the end of Ravel's Second *Daphnis and Chloe* Suite, the trills in the 'Game of Two Rival Cities' section in the *Rite of Spring* by Stravinsky, and even such an early example as the first movement of Handel's *Water Music*.

Another problem for the composer is posed by the dynamic markings for horn parts. Of course, the answer depends upon whether the composer uses *relative* or *absolute* dynamic values. If he uses the latter, the correct dynamic becomes the player's or conductor's problem. My advice—based on much practical experience on *both* sides of the fence—would be to notate in relative dynamics, and to mark the horn part one degree softer than a comparable woodwind part, *except* in the low register (see p. 77).

Nowadays composers seem to be addicted—often rather indiscriminately—to the effect known as 'fluttertongue', an effect produced by fluttering the tongue in a long *rrrrrrr* against the ridge of the gums. On the horn this effect should be used with some caution. It is most successful when used *con sordino*, because it allows the player to fluttertongue with considerable force without becoming overbearing in terms of dynamic level. Composers should realize that a soft fluttertongue on the open horn is extremely difficult or in many instances impossible. A single note, a typical example one is apt to encounter quite often, makes very little sense, since it is virtually impossible to make the fluttertongue speak at such a low dynamic level. And if it should speak, the note is much too short to generate enough *rrrrr*'s to make it worthwhile.

In the low register, the above problem becomes even more acute, and I strongly advise composers to eliminate entirely from their instrumental bag of tricks the flutter-tongue below (sounding) c. At best the effect in that register is quite raucous and splattering. Once again, the trombone has a bore and mouthpiece which make him a much better protagonist of such ideas.

Another suggestion to composers is to consider the fact that horn players have to breathe. I know that it is sometimes a problem to co-ordinate musical inspiration with such technical considerations, but composers should give some thought to this question. It is not impossible to build breathing or resting places into long phrases *during* the actual composing process. It may be easier to just 'let the player worry about it', but often this can lead to unhappy results.

A common fault of modern composers is to write unison passages for all four horns in the extreme high register. This is not wise for two reasons: 1) some exceptions notwithstanding, fourth horn players (and even some second players) are generally not as comfortable in that register as first or third horn players. If they are to meet the normal requirements of low horn writing, they will tend to use a slightly larger mouthpiece, which, in turn, will make the extreme high range more difficult to produce; 2) even if all four players can get these high notes, the intonation is apt to be fairly variable, depending on particular instruments, mouthpieces and individual capacities. Very few players of even otherwise first-rate calibre are able to control the intonation of high notes completely. It is sheer folly to expect *four* players to have that degree of control, especially when two of them have very little experience with that register.

But the problem is more serious than that. When more than one player attempts a high passage at a loud dynamic level, unless their intonation is perfect, a curious phenomenon takes place. The fractional intonational differences set up intense vibrations, vibrations so intense in the immediate vicinity of the players (they lose in impact at a wider range, which is why very few conductors become aware of this problem), that it becomes virtually impossible for any one of the players to sustain his note. That is the reason why one hears so many cracked notes in high register unison horn passages. It is therefore advisable to orchestrate such passages, whenever possible, for first and third horn alone, or to reinforce the two horns with one trumpet.

The acoustical explanation of this disturbing phenomenon is that high notes on a horn create such intensely vibrating air columns, that another player's lips and instrument, if in the immediate vicinity, are *physically* affected. If the same unison passage were attempted with each player sitting ten feet apart, the problem would (for all practical purposes) be eliminated.

A similar plight for the horn player presents itself when he is placed directly in front of a wall or in front of the timpani. Conductors all over the world seem totally unaware of this hazard, and are content to blame the player, when in reality the player is only fighting a losing battle with certain immutable acoustical laws. Boegner conducted experiments which prove decisively that a horn tone, produced directly in front of a solid wall (stone or other extremely hard surfaces are most offensive), will be affected negatively by the wavelengths reflected back from the wall. Boegner's experiments show that the transient time required to produce a given note with its full complement of partials takes considerably longer when played against a wall than when produced in an unobstructed place.

Whatever I have said about the interference of vibrating neighbouring air columns and obstructing surfaces is magnified when the horn player is asked to play in front of the timpani. The impact of the wavelengths generated by a loud timpani note, or worse yet, a loud timpani roll, is so intense, that the player may as well put his horn in his lap and sit it out. The timpani's spreading wavelengths back up through the horn, violently jarring the player's lips. Under these conditions split notes abound and what notes can be played develop a strong rasp. A half a minute of this, and the horn player will retain no sensitivity in his lips. Since the bells of horns face backwards, i.e. invariably towards the timpani, the impact of the timpani on the horn is an extremely direct and painful one.

I have often been asked: 'What makes a horn part a *good* horn part?' I believe if a composer were to consider the suggestions offered in this chapter, he would come quite close to writing logically for the horn. A good horn part is one that is truly *hornistic*, regardless of its difficulty. At the turn of the century, players considered the horn writing of Richard Strauss a monstrous outrage against the instrument. We know now that Strauss's horn writing, except in some of his later works (parts of *Arabella*, *The Silent Woman*, and even his second Horn Concerto), is among the most idiomatic ever conceived. Strauss, the son of one of Europe's greatest horn players of the time (Wagner constantly demanded his services), evidently had a *feeling* for the horn that transcended mere statistical knowledge. And regardless how difficult a given passage in his early works, it is almost always thoroughly hornistic. It takes into consideration the basic sonority and technical characteristics of the horn in such a way that it could not possibly be confused with any other instrument. In fact a solo like the main theme of *Till Eulenspiegel*, with its instinctive adherence to the harmonic series and its wide range, is a superb prototype of inspired horn writing, the horn solo *par excellence*. Indeed, all of Strauss's horn writing adheres to the basic concept of fewer notes and wider skips in the low register (with an emphasis on the first four notes of the harmonic series), and more notes and closer intervals in the upper register.

Of course, composers since then have gone far beyond this ultimately still confining concept. But historically viewed, Strauss's position represented the most advanced solution feasible within the tonal context of his music. It was logical for him to think of the horn as an instrument whose chromatic possibilities were the consequence of a fundamental harmonic series and six easily available 'transpositions' thereof. His style suited this concept perfectly. However, once compositional styles passed beyond tonality to atonality, the horn had to be thought of as a fundamentally chromatic instrument, and Strauss's 'harmonic series' approach lost its validity. This left composers with, on the one hand, greater freedom in the use of the horn, but on the other hand, no rules to follow.

It remained for Schoenberg to evolve a new horn language which was logical and effective because it was in itself no more than an expansion of the chromatic horn writing developed by Wagner in his later operas, and by Mahler. Schoenberg's horn parts in *Gurrelieder*, for example, are a perfect link between late nineteenth-century horn writing and that of his later 'atonal' style. When I once asked Schoenberg how he developed such a feeling for the horn, he gave most of the credit to the Viennese star horn player, Stiegler, who, though he 'fluffed' often on his single F horn, must have been in many respects a most remarkable player. Schoenberg said he was often able to ask Stiegler's advice, and recalled that most of his youthful musical life was in a sense filled with the sound of Stiegler's horn.[1] This feeling for the horn accounts for the astounding fact that the extremely difficult part in Schoenberg's Woodwind Quintet is thoroughly hornistic. By that I mean that a) it derives from a close understanding, intuitive and intellectual, of the

[1] Schoenberg's feeling for orchestration was not limited to the horn, of course, which the foregoing might imply to the casual reader. On the contrary, Schoenberg was in all respects a unique orchestrational innovator, who among other things, opened up new horizons for underdog instruments, such as the trombone and the double bass.

G

intrinsic nature of the horn, and that b) it is a part which could not be anything but a horn part. This may seem like a rather obvious point to make. Yet surely we all know hundreds of examples in contemporary music in which a certain instrumental part could be played without any musical loss on any other instrument capable of the required range. This, it seems to me, is not good orchestration. If we, as composers, write for the horn, we must write a *horn part* or suffer the consequences.

Other twentieth-century composers who have written extremely well for the horn are Stravinsky, Webern, and to a more limited extent Alban Berg. Stravinsky has a special talent for composing fine-sounding high horn parts. They annoy some conservative players, but they almost always sound magnificent. It is a pity that Stravinsky's predilection for the leaner timbres of brass instruments has deterred him from using the horn in his chamber music, the Septet and Four Russian Songs being notable exceptions.

The horn parts in Berg's Violin Concerto could have been written by a horn player. They are an imaginatively rich extension of the chromatic possibilities of the horn. However, in *Wozzeck* and his Chamber Concerto there are a number of passages which seem not to have been as carefully thought out, so that, difficult or easy, they never sound quite right.

Webern seems to have had an immediate grasp of what constitutes good horn writing. Even the extravagant phrases in the first horn part of his opus 1 *Passacaglia* are logical, though quite difficult. They are a challenge to the player and a source of great satisfaction when well performed. But even the exceedingly advanced horn writing in Webern's Symphony, op. 21, is completely idiomatic. One has only to ask oneself if those parts could be played as effectively on any other instrument. The answer is a decided no. Both the first and second parts represent a real understanding of the horn sonority in its entire range. They also run the gamut of expression, from the lyrical to the brash and explosive. Although the bassoon, trombone, and cello have the range required to perform these parts, not a single note by any one of these instruments could be substituted in their stead without considerable loss of musical validity.

A word of caution might be apropos at this point: not everything in nineteenth-century horn writing is to be considered an infallible source. The famous horn solo from the second movement of Franck's symphony, while mastered nowadays by any self-respecting first horn player, does not represent the most logical way to use the horn. The solo lies in a strange key—a half tone lower it would present many less difficulties—and is made more problematical by the fact that it is scored at a low dynamic level, blending in unison with the clarinet who—to further compound the problems—is playing in a clarinet register in which the intonation of certain notes is extremely hard to control. Needless to say, if the horn player favours the clarinettist's intonational solutions, he endangers his own accuracy.

The trio of Schumann's Rhenish Symphony is another first horn part that composers should not accept as a criterion of idiomatic orchestral horn writing. This passage looks quite reasonable on paper, but a combination of circumstances conspire to render it one of the more unnerving experiences in the horn literature. It is a little lengthy, a little repetitious, and in its orchestrational setting, just a little too exposed. A player will give his all getting one or two high C's in a passage, but when a composer asks him to produce that C four or more times, he is really pushing his luck.

Further examples of horn writing that is at best very specialized, and therefore not to be taken as either the most effective or most logical way to use the horn, are: Berlioz's *Queen Mab* Scherzo and most of Verdi's horn writing (especially the opening of the third act of *Don Carlos*). From the point of view of endurance, I should like to cite *The*

Flying Dutchman and *Lohengrin* as examples of horn parts not to be emulated. Whereas *Tristan, Die Meistersinger*, and *The Ring* are certainly problematic in terms of endurance, the horn writing in these works is at least consistently effective, and indeed could not be duplicated by any other instruments. In the two above-mentioned earlier examples, however, the horn parts are extremely tiring, and yet rarely of great musical import, being often no more than a kind of 'super' second violin parts.

The best and surest approach to learning something about the horn is to spend some actual time with a fine player who has an open mind—some of the more cynical hide-bound professionals being no help in this respect. The suggestion that composers actually experiment for a few days or weeks on a horn is dangerous, since it often leads to a situation where 'a little knowledge is worse than none'. A few days of 'dabbling' with the horn cannot approximate the sound advice a first-rate professional player might impart. And in closing I should like to add that, by and large, horn players are a fairly intelligent, patient, and accommodating lot. The fearsome difficulties of the instrument almost demand these qualities.

REPERTOIRE LIST

The following list consists of works which the author believes will be of interest to horn players. As such, extensive though it is, it makes no attempt to be definitively complete. It includes not only works in which the horn is treated soloistically, but also chamber music repertoire in which the horn writing is challenging, musically and technically.

Lesser-known compositions marked * indicate the author's opinion that such works are in one way or another of special interest. Works marked ** are believed to be out of print, and may require some search in libraries and antiquarian shops. When no publisher is given and no ** appears, the work is well-established public domain material available in many editions. In the few cases where a publisher is not given and ** does appear, editions not specifically known to the compiler exist, but are believed to be out of print.

The list is arranged as follows:

Horn and Piano

One Horn or Ensemble of Horns (basically without other instruments)
- a)   One Horn
- b)   Two Horns
- c)   Three Horns
- d)   Four Horns
- e)   Five or more Horns

Horn and Orchestra (including Horn in Concertante works, with or without other instruments; also more than one Horn with Orchestra)

Chamber Music
- a)   Two, Three, or Four Instruments
- b)   Five Instruments
- c)   Six to Nine Instruments
- d)   Ten or more Instruments

ABBREVIATIONS

A.C.A.	American Composer's Alliance, New York
A.M.P.	Associated Music Publishers, New York
B. & H.	Boosey and Hawkes
Breitkopf	Breitkopf & Härtel
E.M.	Edition Modern, Munich
Hudebni	Hudebni Matice, Prague
Morris	Edwin Morris, New York
P.W.M.	Polski Wydawnictwo Muzyczne, Warsaw (represented by Musica Rara in London)
Pro Musica	Pro Musica Verlag, Leipzig
R.S.P.H.	Russian State Publishing House (represented by Musica Rara in London, and by Leeds Music in New York)
S.M.	Skandinavsk Musikforlag, Copenhagen
S.P.A.M.	Society for the Publication of American Music (Fischer, N.Y.)
U.E.	Universal Edition
Zerboni	Suvini-Zerboni, Milano

Picc.	Piccolo	Timp.	Timpani
Fl.	Flute	Perc.	Percussion
Ob.	Oboe	Hp.	Harp
EH.	English Horn	Pno.	Piano
E flat Cl.	E flat Clarinet	Cel.	Celesta
Cl.	Clarinet	Vib.	Vibraphone
Bs. Cl.	Bass Clarinet	Gtr.	Guitar
Bn.	Bassoon	Dr.	Drums
C. Bn.	Contra Bassoon	Vn.	Violin
Hn.	French Horn	Va.	Viola
Tpt.	Trumpet	Vc.	Cello
Tromb.	Trombone	Db.	Doublebass
Bari. Hn.	Baritone Horn	Str. Quart.	String Quartet
Alt. Sax.	Alto Saxophone	WW. Quint.	Woodwind Quintet
Ten. Sax.	Tenor Saxophone	Str. Trio.	String Trio (Vn., Va., Vc.)
Bsst. Hn.	Bassethorn	Str. Quint.	String Quintet (2 Vn., Va., Vc., Db.)

HORN AND PIANO

Alexandrov, Y.	Three Pieces	R.S.P.H.
b. 1914		
Bassett, L.	Sonata	Morris, N.Y.
b. 1923		
Beck, C.	Intermezzo	Heugel
b. 1901		
Beethoven, L. v.	Sonata	
b. 1772		
Bentzon, N. V.	Sonata	Hansen
b. 1919		
Bernstein, L.	Elegy for Mippy	Schirmer
b. 1918		
Beversdorf, T.	Sonata	Andraud,
b. 1924		Cincinnati
Bozza, E.	En Forêt	Leduc
b. 1905		
Bruneau, A.	Romance	Hamelle
b. 1857	Fantasie	Choudens
Bush, A.	Autumn Poem	Schott
b. 1900	Trent's Broad Reaches	Schott
Campolieti, L.	Andante Pastorale and Allegro	Ricordi
Carse, A.	Serenade and Scherzino	Augener
b. 1878		
Chabrier, E.	Larghetto	Costallat
b. 1841		
Cooke, A.	Rondo	Schott
b. 1906		
Cortese, L.	Sonata	Carisch
b. 1899		
Coscia, S.	Romanza	M. Baron, N.Y.
Danzi, F.	Sonata	Sikorski
b. 1763	Sonata	Hofmeister
Delamarter, E.	Ballade and Poème	Remick, N.Y.
b. 1880		
Donato, A.	Sonata	Remick, N.Y.
b. 1909		
Draesecke, F.	Adagio, Romanze	**Kistner
b. 1835		
Dukas, P.	Vilanelle	Durand
b. 1865		

HORN AND PIANO (*cont.*)

Finke, F. b. 1891	Sonata	Breitkopf
Fricker, P. R. b. 1920	Sonata	Schott
Gabelles, G.	Fantasie	Alfred, N.Y.
Glazounov, A. b. 1865	Reverie	Belaieff
Gliere, R. b. 1875	Nocturne	R.S.P.H.
Grant, W. P. b. 1910	Mirror and Ostinato (Hn. and Org.)	A.C.A., N.Y.
Haas, J. b. 1879	Sonata	Schott
Hamilton, I. b. 1922	Aria	Schott
Heiden, B. b. 1910	Sonata	A.M.P., N.Y.
Henselt, A. b. 1814	Duo for Hn. and Pno.	**Cranz, Hambur
Hindemith, P. b. 1895	Sonata	Schott
Hlobil, E. b. 1901	Andante Pastorale	Bärenreiter
Horn, K. b. 1860	Sonata	**Kahnt, Leipzig
Ivanov, Y.	Duet for 2 Hns. and Pno.	R.S.P.H.
Kaminski, H. b. 1886	Ballade	Bärenreiter
Kauder, H. b. 1888	Sonata 2 Sonatas	B. &. H. *MS.*
Korn, P.	Sonata	Simrock
Koslovsky, J. b. 1757	*Romance	R.S.P.H.
Krol, B. b. 1920	Sonata	Pro Musica, Leipzig
Le Flem, P. b. 1881	Pièce	Eschig
Leroux, X. b. 1863	Sonata	Leduc
Lindpaintner, P. b. 1791	Variations and Rondo	**Breitkopf
Makarov, E. b. 1912	Romance	R.S.P.H.

HORN AND PIANO (*cont.*)

Mihalovici, M.	Episode	Leduc
b. 1898		
Moser, R.	Sonata	**Steingräber
b. 1892		
Mouret, J. J.	*Deux Divertissements	Ed. du Siècle
b. 1682		Musical Geneva
Mulder, H.	Sonata	Donemus
b. 1898		
Nielsen, C.	Canto Serioso	S.M.
b. 1865		
Nowak, L.	Sonata	A.C.A., N.Y.
b. 1911		
Orr, R.	Serenade	Schott
b. 1909		
Pisk, P.	Sonata	A.C.A., N.Y.
b. 1893		
Poot, M.	Legende	Leduc
b. 1901		
Porter, Q.	Sonata	Gamble, Chicago
b. 1897		
Poser, H.	Sonata	Sikorski
Poulenc, F.	Elegie	Chester
b. 1899		
Raff, J.	Zwei Romanzen	**Siegel, Leipzig
b. 1822		
Ravel, M.	Pavane	Eschig
b. 1875		
Read, G.	Poem	Fischer, N. Y.
b. 1913		
Rheinberger, J.	Sonata	**Kistner, Leipzig
b. 1839		
Ries, F.	Sonata	**Richault, Paris
b. 1784		
Rossini, G.	Prelude, Theme and Variations	Rossini Foundation, Pesaro
b. 1792		
Schibler, A.	Prologue, Invocation et Danse	Ahn & Simrock, Berlin
b. 1920		
Schreiter, H.	Sonatina	Bote & Bock
b. 1915		
Schuller, G.	Nocturne	Mills
b. 1925		
Schumann, R.	Adagio and Allegro	
b. 1810		

HORN AND PIANO (*cont.*)

Scriabin, A. b. 1872	Romance	U.E.
Sikorski, K. b. 1895	Concerto	P.W.M., Warsaw
Sinigaglia, L. b. 1868	Lied and Humoresque	Breitkopf
Spindler, F. b. 1817	Sonata	**Siegel, Leipzig
Stevens, H. b. 1908	Sonata	Morris, N.Y.
Strauss, F. b. 1822	Nocturne	U.E.
Verall, J. b. 1908	Sonata	*MS*
Vignieri	Sonata Op. 7	R.S.P.H.
Walker, E. b. 1870	Adagio	Williams
Wilder, A. b. 1907	Sonata	*MS.*
Wilm, N. b. 1834	Romanze and Scherzo	**Forberg, Leipzig
Windsperger, L. b. 1885	Pieces for Horn	Schott
Ziring, V. b. 1880	Adagio	R.S.P.H.

ONE HORN OR HORN ENSEMBLE

1) ONE HORN

Raphling, S. b. 1910	Sonata	
Wellesz, E. b. 1885	Fanfare	Ed. Musicus, N.Y.

2) TWO HORNS

	Collection of Original Duets from 18th and 19th Century	Hofmeister
André, J. A. b. 1775	Twelve Pieces	**André, Offenbach
Brahms, J. b. 1833	Four Songs for Women's Voices, Hp. and 2 Hns.	**Simrock; Musica Rara

ONE HORN OR HORN ENSEMBLE (*cont.*)

Cobb, S.	Sonatina	Fischer, N.Y.
Dauprat, L. F.	Twenty Duos	**Lemoine
b. 1781		
Flothuis, M.	Three Pieces	Donemus
b. 1914		
Ivanov, Y.	Duet for 2 Horns and Piano	R.S.P.H.
Mozart, W. A.	Twelve Duos	McGinnis &
b. 1756		Marx, N.Y.
Nicolai, O.	*Duet	Musica Rara,
b. 1810		London
Rasmussen, P.	Duets	Hansen
Rimsky-	*Two Duets	Musica Rara
Korsakov, G.		
b. 1844		

3) THREE HORNS

Beethoven, L. v.	*Quintet (3 Hns., Ob., Bn.)	Schott
b. 1770		
Cowell, H.	Hymn and Fuguing Tune	A.M.P., N.Y.
b. 1897	No. 12	
Dauprat, L. F.	Trios	**Lemoine
b. 1781		
Reicha, A.	Six Trios	Merseburger;
b. 1770		Forberg
Schneider, G. A.	18 Trios	Pro Musica
b. 1770		
Villa-Lobos, H.	*Chorôs No. 4 (3 Hns., Tromb.)	Eschig
b. 1887		

4) FOUR HORNS

Becher, H.	Sinfonietta	Grosch, Dortmund
Bozza, E.	Suite	Leduc
b. 1905		
Castelnuovo-	Chorale and Variations	**
Tedesco, M.		
b. 1895		
Coscia, S.	Suite	M. Baron, N.Y.
Dauprat, L. F.	Quartets	**Lemoine
b. 1781		
Graas, J.	Three Quartets	Mills
b. 1924		
Griend,	Quartet	Donemus
K. van de		
b. 1905		

ONE HORN OR HORN ENSEMBLE (*cont.*)

Hindemith, P. b. 1895	Sonata for Four Horns	Schott
Kienzl, W. b. 1857	3 Konzertstücke	**Oertel, Hanover
Koetsier, J. b. 1911	Petite Suite	Donemus
McKay, F. b. 1899	Two Pieces	Gamble, Chicago
Mityushin, A. b. 1888	Concertino for Horn Quartet	R.S.P.H.
Ochs, R. b. 1887	Vergnügliche Musik	Pro Musica
Otey, W. b. 1914	Prelude, Scherzo and Passa- caglia	Sansone, N.Y.
Poldini, E. b. 1869	Serenade	U.E.
Rimsky- Korsakov, G. b. 1844	*Notturno	Musica Rara
Schuller, G. b. 1925	Quintet for 4 Hns. and Bn. (Tuba)	MJQ Music, N.Y.
Schumann, R. b. 1810	Gesänge (Male Chorus and 4 Hns.)	Peters
Stravinsky, I. b. 1882	Four Russian Choruses (Women's Voices and 4 Hns.)	B. &. H.
Suttner, J. b. 1881	4 Quartets	Grosch, Dort- mund
Tippett, M. b. 1905	Sonata for Four Horns	Schott
Tscherepnin, N. b. 1873	*Six Quartets	Belaieff
Wilder, A. b. 1907	*Serenade (and other Pieces) 4 Hns, Harpsichord, Bass and Drums	MJQ Music, N.Y.
Windsperger, L. b. 1885	Three Suites	Schott
Zbinden, J. F. b. 1917	*Three Pieces	Breitkopf

5) LARGE HORN ENSEMBLES

Schuller, G. b. 1925	Five Pieces for Five Horns	MJQ Music, N.Y.

ONE HORN OR HORN ENSEMBLE *(cont.)*

Dauprat, L. F. b. 1781	Sextets for Horns	**Lemoine
Schuller, G. b. 1925	Lines and Contrasts (for 16 Hns.)	MJQ Music, N.Y.

HORN AND ORCHESTRA†

(†One horn and full orchestra, unless otherwise stated.)

André, J. A. b. 1775	Concerto	**André, Offen- bach
	Double Concerto (2 Hns. and Orch.)	**André, Offen- bach
Alinovi, G. b. 1790	Divertimento	**Ricordi
Amram, D. b. 1930	Concerto (Ob., 2 Hns., Str.)	*MS.*
Arnold, M. b. 1921	Concerto	Lengnick
Atterberg, K. b. 1887	*Concerto	Breitkopf
Bach, J. S. b. 1685	Brandenburg Concerto No. 1 (2 Hns., 3 Obs., Vln., Str. and Cont.)	
Bachelet, A. b. 1864	*Lamento (Hn. and Str.)	Leduc
Becker, J. b. 1886	Concerto	**New Music, N.Y.
Bennet, R. b. 1936	Concerto	U.E.
Blacher, B. b. 1903	Concerto (Hn,. Cl., Bn., Tpt., Hp. and Str.)	Bote and Bock
Borresen, H. b. 1876	Serenade for Hn., Str. and Timp.	Dania, Kopen- Hagen
Brandt-Buys, J. b. 1868	Suite (Hn., Hp. and Str.)	**Cranz, Hamburg
Britten, B. b. 1913	Serenade for Tenor, Hn. and Strings	B. & H.
Chabrier, E. b. 1841	Larghetto	Costallat; Salabert
Chavez, C. b. 1899	*Concerto for Four Hns. and Orchestra	Schirmer, N.Y.
Coscia, S.	Concertino	M. Baron, N.Y.

HORN AND ORCHESTRA *(cont.)*

Danzi, F. b. 1763	Sinfonia Concertante (Fl., Ob., Hn., Bn. and Orch.)	Schott
Dimmler, A. b. 1753	Concertante (2 Hns, and Orch.)	Ars Viva-Scott
Eckert, F.	Concerto	**U.E.
Flothuis, M. b. 1914	Concerto	Donemus
Foerster, Chr. b. 1693	Concerto (Hn. and Str.)	Hofmeister
Franz, O. b. 1843	Konzertstück for 2 Hns and Orch.	Sansone, N.Y.
Gal, H. b. 1890	Fantasies (Contralto, Cl., Hn., Hp., Str.)	U.E.
Gavazzeni, G. b. 1909	Piccolo Concerto (Fl., Hn. and Str.)	Casa Musicale, Giuliana, Trieste
Ghedini, G. F. b. 1892	Concerto Grosso (WW. Quint. and Orch.)	Zerboni
Gillmann, K.	Concerto	Grahl, Apolda (E. Germany)
Glazounov, A. b. 1865	Reverie	Belaieff
Gliere, R. b. 1875	Concerto	R.S.P.H.; Ricordi
Gluck, Ch. W. b. 1714	*Sinfonia (2 Hns., Str.)	U.E.
Gödicke, A. F. b. 1877	Concerto	**U.E.
Grandjany, M. b. 1891	Poeme (Hn., Hp. and Orch.)	*MS.*
Handel, G. F. b. 1685	*Concerto (2 Wind Choirs and Strings)	Breitkopf
Haydn, J. b. 1732	Cassation (4 Hns. and Str.) Cassation (2 Hns. and Str.) Two Concerti Horn Signal Symphony, No. 31 (Four very soloistic horn parts)	Doblinger Vieweg Breitkopf
Hindemith, P. b. 1895	Concertino	Schott
Huggler, J. b. 1928	*Concerto (Hn. and Str.)	Leeds, N.Y.

HORN AND ORCHESTRA (*cont.*)

Jacob, G. b. 1895	Concerto (Hn. and Str.)	Williams, London
Kaun, B.	Sinfonia Concertante	Jupiter, Holly- wood
Kayser, L.	Concerto	**
Kiel, A.	Concerto	**Oertel, Hanover
Klebe, G. b. 1925	*Espressione Liriche (Hn., Tpt., Tromb. and Orch.)	Schott,-U.E.
Kling, H.	Concerto	**Oertel, Hanover
Komarovsky, A. b. 1909	Concerto	R.S.P.H.
Korn, P.	Concerto	*MS.*
Koslovsky, J. b. 1757	*Romance	R.S.P.H.
Kox, H. b. 1930	Concertante Musik (Hn., Tpt., Tromb. and Orch.)	Donemus
Kuhlau, F. b. 1786	*Concertino for 2 Hns. and Orch.	**Schmidt, Heil- bronn
Larsson, L. b. 1908	Divertimento (WW. Quint., Str.)	U.E.
Leschetizky, T. b. 1830	*Scherzo for Hn. and Orch.	U.E.
Luening, O. b. 1900	Serenade (3 Hns. and Orch.)	A.C.A., N.Y.
Lutyens, E. b. 1906	Concerto	Chester
Martelli, H. b. 1895	Concertino (Ob., Cl., Bn., Hn. and Str.)	Ricordi
Martin, F. b. 1890	*Concerto for 7 Winds and Str.	U.E.
Matisse, K.	Two Concertos	R.S.P.H.
Mendelssohn, F. b. 1809	Nocturne (from Midsummer Night's Dream)	
Mengelberg, K. b. 1902	Concerto	Donemus
Mozart, L. b. 1719	Concerto (Hn., Vn. and Orch.) *Sinfonia di Caccia (4 Hns., Str.)	Breitkopf U.E.
Mozart, W. A. b. 1756	Four Concerti Concert Rondo Sinfonia Concertante (Ob., Cl., Bn., Hn. and Orch.)	
Müller, Fr. b. 1786	Concertante (Cl., Hn. and Orch.)	Breitkopf

HORN AND ORCHESTRA (*cont.*)

Norden, H. b. 1909	Passacaglia (Hn. and Str.)	Chester
Pauwels, E. b. 1768	Concerto	**Wiessenbruch, Brussels
Pleyel, I. b. 1757	Several Sinfonie Concertante for Winds and Orch.	**Sieber
Quinet, M. b. 1915	Sinfonietta (WW. Quint., Timp., Str.)	U.E.
Rawsthorne, A. b. 1905	Concertante Pastorale (Fl. Hn. and Str.)	O.U.P.
Rieti, V. b. 1898	Concerto (WW. Quint. and Orch.)	U.E.
Rogers, B. b. 1893	Fantasia for Solo Hn., Timp. and Str.	Presser, Bryn Mawr, Penn.
Rosetti, A. b. 1750	Concerto (E flat)	Simrock; N.Y. Public Library
	Concerto (B flat)	Hofmeister
Saint-Saens, C. b. 1835	Morceau de Concert (Hn. and Str.	Durand
	Romance	Durand
Schoeck, O. b. 1886	*Concerto	B. & H.
Schuller, G. b. 1925	Concerto	MJQ Music, N.Y.
Schumann, R. b. 1810	Adagio and Allegro (Instr. by E. Ansermet)	U.E.
	*Konzertstück for 4 Hns. and Orch.	Breitkopf
Searle, H. b. 1915	Aubade (Hn. and Str.)	Schott
Seiber, M. b. 1905	*Notturno (Hn. and Str.)	Schott
Shebalin, V. b. 1902	Concertino	R.S.P.H.
Smyth, E. b. 1858	Concerto (Vn., Hn. and Orch.)	Curwen
Stamitz, K. b. 1745	*Sinfonia Concertante (Vn., Vc., Fl.,Ob., Cl., 2 Hns. and Orch.)	U.E.
Strauss, F. b. 1822	Concerto	U.E.
	Nocturne	U.E.
	Romanze	U.E.
Strauss, R. b. 1864	Concerto No. 1	
	Concerto No. 2	B. & H.

HORN AND ORCHESTRA (*cont.*)

Telemann, G. P. b. 1681	*Concerto (2 Hns., Str. and Cont.)	Breitkopf
Toldi, J.	Concerto	Ars Viva-Schott
Tomasi, H. b. 1901	Concerto	Leduc
Tomlinson, E. b. 1924	Rhapsody and Rondo	Mills
Van den Broeck, O. b. 1759	Concerto	**
Vivaldi, A. b. 1677	2 Concerti (2 Hns. and Str.)	Ricordi
Weber, C. M. b. 1786	Concertino	
Webern, A. b. 1883	*Sinfonie (Cl., Bs. Cl., 2 Hns., Hp. and Str.)	U.E.
Wilder, A. b. 1907	Concerto	*MS.*
Wolf-Ferrari, E. b. 1876	Concertino (Ob., 2 Hns. and Str.)	Ricordi
Woltmann, F. b. 1908	Poem (Hn. and Str.) Rhapsody	*MS.* *MS.*
Zelenka, J. D. b. 1681	Caprice	**

CHAMBER MUSIC

1) TWO, THREE OR FOUR INSTRUMENTS

Addison, J. b. 1920	Divertimento (2 Tpts., Hn., Bari. Hn.)	Mills
Andriessen, H. b. 1892	Aubade (2 Tpt., Hn., Tromb.)	Donemus
Amram, D. b. 1930	Trio (Hn., Bn., Ten. Sax.)	*MS.*
Apostel, H. E. b. 1901	*Quartet (Fl., Cl., Bn., Hn.)	U.E.
Bentzon, J. b. 1897	Symfonisk Trio (Hn., Vn., Db.)	Kistner
Berkeley, L. b. 1903	Trio (Vn., Hn., Pno.)	Chester
Birtwistle, H. b. 1934	Monody for Corpus Christi (Soprano, Fl., Vn., Hn.)	U.E.

H

CHAMBER MUSIC (*cont.*)

Boedijn, G. b. 1893	Quartet (2 Tpts., Hn., Tromb.)	Donemus
Bozza, E. b. 1905	Sonatina (2 Tpts., Hn., Tromb.)	Leduc
Brahms, J. b. 1833	Trio (Vn., Hn., Pno.)	
Casanova, A. b. 1919	*Trio (Fl., Hn., Va.)	Bomart, N.Y.
Dessau, P. b. 1894	*Concertino (Vn., Fl., Cl., Hn.)	Schott
Di Domenica, R. b. 1927	*Quartet for Fl., Vn., Hn., Pno.	MJQ Music, N.Y.
Dobrzynski, I. F. b. 1807	Duet for Cl. and Hn.	P.W.M., Warsaw
Flothuis, M. b. 1914	Sonatina (Hn., Tpt., Tromb.)	Donemus
Gal, H. b. 1890	Fantasies (Contralto, Cl., Hn., Pno.)	U.E.
Glazounov, A. b. 1865	Serenade No. 2 (Hn. and Str. Quart.)	R.S.P.H.
	Idyll (Hn. and Str. Quart.)	R.S.P.H.
Handel, G. F. b. 1685	*Sonata for 2 Cls. and Hn.	Schott; Mercury, N.Y.
Haydn, J. b. 1732	Trio (Hn., Vn., Vc., Cont.)	U.E.; Doblinger
	Twelve Nocturnes (2 Fls., 2 Hns.)	Pro Musica
	Divertimento No. 5 (2 Cls., 2 Hns.)	Hansen; Doblinger
	Cassation (2 Fls., 2 Hns.)	Ars Viva-Schott
Haydn, M. b. 1737	Divertimento (Fl., Ob., Bn., Hn.)	Hofmeister
Herzogen-berg, H. b. 1843	Trio (Ob., Hn., Pno.)	**Biedermann, Leipzig
Holbrooke, J. b. 1878	Trio (Vn., Hn., Pno.)	**Rudall & Carte, London
Hovhaness, A. b. 1911	Divertimento (Ob., Cl., Bn., Hn.)	Peters-Hinrichsen
Huber, K. b. 1924	Des Engels Anrufung (Fl., Cl., Hn., Hp.)	U.E.
Jacob, G. b. 1895	Scherzo (2 Tpts., Hn., Bari. Hn.)	Lengnick-Mills
Jacobsohn, G. b. 1923	Adagio and Allegro (Ob., Cl., Hn.)	Israeli Music, Tel Aviv

CHAMBER MUSIC (*cont.*)

Kauder, H.	Trio (Vn., Hn., Pno.)	B. & H.
b. 1888	Quartet (Ob., Cl., Bn., Hn.)	**New Music, N.Y.
Kohs, E.	*Night Watch (Fl., Hn., Timp.)	A.C.A., N.Y.
b. 1916		
Krejci, I.	Divertimento (Fl., Cl., Bn.,	Hudebni
b. 1904	Hn.)	
Kupferman, M.	*Curtain Raiser (Fl., Cl., Hn.,	*MS.*
b. 1926	Pno.)	
Lucas, L.	Aubade (Hn., Bn., Pno.)	Chester
b. 1903		
Luening, O.	Short Fantasy (Vn., Hn.)	A.C.A., N.Y.
b. 1900		
Poulenc, F.	*Sonate (Hn., Tpt., Tromb.)	Chester
b. 1899		
Ramsoe, W.	4 Quartets (Cornet, Tpt., Hn.,	Hansen
b. 1837	Tuba)	
Raphael, G.	Sonatina (Vn., Bn., Hn.)	Breitkopf
b. 1903		
Reinecke, K.	Trio (Ob., Hn., Pno.)	Breitkopf
b. 1824	Trio (Cl., Hn., Pno.)	Breitkopf
Rossini, G.	Six Quartets (Fl., Cl., Bn., Hn.)	Ricordi; Schott
b. 1792		
Rust, F. W.	Sonata (Va., 2 Hns., Vc.,	Pro Musica
b. 1739	[Cont?]	
Schubert, F.	Auf dem Strom (Soprano, Hn.,	
b. 1797	Pno.)	
Schuller, G.	Trio (Ob., Hn., Va.)	MJQ Music,
b. 1925		N.Y.
Stamitz, K.	*Quartet (Ob., Hn., Va. or Cl.,	Breitkopf;
b. 1745	Bn. or Vc.)	Leuckart
Stich, W.	Two Quartets (Hn., Vn., Va.,	Bärenreiter
b. 1746	Vc.)	
Stölzel, G. H.	*Sonata (Ob., Hn., Vn., Cont.)	Breitkopf
b. 1690		
Tovey, D. F.	Trio (Cl., Hn., Pno.)	Schott
b. 1875		
Ullrich, H. J.	Fantasy Trio (Vn., Hn., Pno.)	M. & H. Publish-
b. 1888		ing, Flushing,
		N.Y.
Wildgans, F.	3 Inventions (Cl., Hn.)	Doblinger
b. 1913		
Zelenka, I.	Trio (Vn., Hn., Pno.)	E.M.
b. 1936		

H*

CHAMBER MUSIC (cont.)

2) FIVE INSTRUMENTS†

†Unless otherwise indicated works are for
Fl., Ob., Cl., Bn., Hn.

Andriessen, H. b. 1892	Quintet	Donemus
Aschen- brenner, T. b. 1903	Quintet	E.M.
Badings, H. b. 1907	Quintet	Donemus
Barber, S. b. 1910	Summer Music	Schirmer, N.Y.
Beethoven, L. v. b. 1772	Quintet (Ob., Cl., Bn., Hn., Pno.)	
	Quintet (Ob., 3 Hns., Bn.)	Schott
Berezowsky, N. b. 1900	Suite No. 2 for WW. Quint.	Mills
Bergsma, W. b. 1921	Concerto (WW. Quint.)	Galaxy, N.Y.
Bozza, E. b. 1905	Variations sur un Thème Libre	Leduc
Brod, H. b. 1801	*Quintet	McGinnis & Marx, N.Y.
	Quintet	**Lemoine
Carter, E. b. 1908	*Quintet	A.M.P., N.Y.
Cherubini, L. b. 1760	Sonata (Hn. and Str. Quart.)	Sikorski
Constant, M. b. 1925	4 Etudes de Concert (2 Hns., Tpt., Tromb., Perc.)	Leduc
Cowell, H. b. 1897	*Suite	A.M.P., N.Y.
Crawford- Seeger, R. b. 1901	*Suite	MS.
Dahl, I. b. 1912	Allegro and Arioso Music for Brass Instruments (2 Tpts., Hn., 2 Trombs.)	MS. Witmark, N.Y.
Danzi, F. b. 1763	Two Quintets (B flat and G) Quintet (Ob., Cl., Bn., Hn., Pno.)	Leuckart Musica Rara, London

CHAMBER MUSIC (*cont.*)

Dauprat, L. F.	3 Quintets (Hn. and Str.)	**Schonenberger,
b. 1781		Paris
Dittersdorf, D. v.	3 Partitas (2 Obs., 2 Hns., Bn.)	Breitkopf
b. 1739		
Douglas, R.	6 Dance Caricatures	Hinrichsen
b. 1907		
Draesecke, F.	Quintet (Hn., Vn., Va., Vc.,	**Kistner
b. 1835	Pno.)	
Eder, H.	Quintet	Doblinger
b. 1916		
Essex, K.	Quintet	Hinrichsen
Etler, A.	Quintet	A.M.P., N.Y.
b. 1913		
Fernandez, O.	Quintet	A.M.P., N.Y.
b. 1897		
Fine, I.	*Partita	B. & H.
b. 1914		
Finke, F.	Quintet	Breitkopf
b. 1891		
Foerster, J. B.	*Quintet	Hudebni
b. 1859		
Fortner, W.	*5 Bagatellen	Schott
b. 1907		
Francaix, J.	*Quintet	Schott
b. 1912		
Fricker, P. R.	Quintet	Schott
b. 1920		
Furst, P. W.	Konzertante Musik	Doblinger
b. 1926		
Füssl, H.	Kleine Kammermusik	Bärenreiter
b. 1924		
Genzmer, H.	Quintet	Litolff
b. 1909		
Gerhard, R.	*Quintet	Hinrichsen
b. 1896		
Gerster, O.	Quintet	Schott
b. 1897		
Gieseking, W.	Quintet (Ob., Cl., Bn., Hn.,	Breitkopf
b. 1895	Pno.)	
Goeb, R.	Quintet	A.C.A., N.Y.
b. 1914		
Hamerik, E.	Quintet	Edition Dania
b. 1898		

CHAMBER MUSIC (*cont.*)

Haydn, J. b. 1732	7 Divertimenti (2 Obs., 2 Hns., Bn.)	Doblinger
Heiden, B. b. 1910	Quintet (Hn. and Str. Quart.) Sinfonia for WW. Quintet	A.M.P., N.Y. A.M.P., N.Y.
Henkemans, H. b. 1913	Quintet	Donemus
Henze, H. W. b. 1926	Quintet	Schott
Hosmer, J.	Fugue in C	Gamble, Chicago
Hindemith b. 1895	Kleine Kammermusik	Schott
Ibert, J. b. 1890	Trois Pièces Brèves	Leduc
Jacob, G. b. 1895	Quintet	B. & H.
Jacoby, H. b. 1909	Quintet	Israeli Music, Tel Aviv
Jersild, J. b. 1913	Serenade	Hansen
Jongen, J. b. 1873	Concerto	Andraud, Cincinnati
Kaminski, H. b. 1886	Quintet (Cl., Hn., Str. Trio)	U.E.
Kelterborn, R. b. 1931	Seven Bagatelles	E.M.
Kubizek, A. b. 1918	Quintet	Doblinger
Landré, G. b. 1905	Quintet	Donemus
Lefèbvre, C. E. b. 1843	Quintet	Hamelle
Leibowitz, R. b. 1913	*Quintet	U.E.
Lessard, J. b. 1920	Partita	A.C.A., N.Y.
Malipiero, G. F. b. 1882	Dialogue No. 4	Ricordi
Malipiero, R. b. 1914	Quintet	Zerboni
Martinu, B. b. 1890	Quintet	Chester
Milhaud, D. b. 1892	La Cheminée du Roi René	Andraud, Cincinnati

CHAMBER MUSIC (*cont.*)

Moore, D.	Quintet	Schirmer
b. 1893		
Mortensen, O.	Quintet	Hansen
b. 1907		
Mozart, W. A.	Quintet (Hn., Vn., 2 Vas., Vc.)	
b. 1756	Quintet (Ob., Cl., Bn., Hn., Pno.)	
Nelhybel, V.	Quintet	Peters
b. 1919		
Nielsen, C.	Serenato Invano (Cl., Bn., Hn., Vc., Db.)	S.M.
b. 1865	*Quintet (Ob. doubles EH)	Hansen
Onslow, G.	Quintet	**Kistner; Leuckart
b. 1784		
Perle, G.	Quintet	A.C.A., N.Y.
b. 1915		
Persichetti, V.	Pastorale	Schirmer
b. 1915		
Pijper, W.	Quintet	Donemus
b. 1894		
Piston, W.	Quintet	A.M.P., N.Y.
b. 1894		
Powell, M.	Divertimento for 5 Winds	S.P.A.M.
b. 1923		
Rameau-Desormière	*Suite from Acante et Céphise	Leduc
b. 1683		
Rathaus, K.	Serenade	B. & H.
b. 1895		
Reicha, A.	Quintet (Hn. and Str. Quart.)	Breitkopf
b. 1770	*24 WW. Quintets	**Simrock; Leuckart
Reizenstein, F.	Quintet	B. & H.
b. 1911		
Riegger, W.	Quintet	Ars Viva-Schott
b. 1885		
Rimsky-Korsakov, G.	Quintet (Fl., Cl., Bn., Hn., Pno.)	Belaieff
b. 1844		
Ropartz, G.	*Deux Pièces	Durand
b. 1864		

HORN TECHNIQUE

CHAMBER MUSIC (*cont.*)

Rota, N. b. 1911	Petite Offrande Musicale	Leduc
Ruynemann, D. b. 1886	Divertimento (Fl., Cl., Hn., Va., Pno.)	Chester
Schindler, G. b. 1921	Divertimento Notturno	E.M.
Schiske, K. b. 1916	Quintet	Doblinger
Schmid, H. K. b. 1874	Quintet	Schott
Schoenberg, A. b. 1874	*Quintet	U.E.
Schuller, G. b. 1925	Quintet	Schott
	Suite	McGinnis & Marx, N.Y.
	Quintet (2 Tpts., Hn., Tromb., Tuba)	Schott
	Quintet for Muted Hns. and Bn. (opt. Tuba)	MJQ Music, N.Y.
Schumann, R. b. 1810	Andante and Variations (Hn., 2 Vcs., 2 Pnos.)	Breitkopf
Seiber, M. b. 1905	*Permutazione a Cinque	Schott
Shapey, R. b. 1921	*Movements	A.C.A., N.Y.
	*De Profundis (Solo Db., Fl., Ob. [EH], Cl. [Bs. Cl., Alt. Sax.], Hn.)	Leeds, N.Y.
Shifrin, S. b. 1926	*Serenade (Ob., Cl., Hn., Va., Pno.)	Litolff
Sinigaglia, L. b. 1868	Romanze (Hn., Str. Quart.)	Ricordi
Sowerby, L. b. 1895	Quintet	Schirmer
Spohr, L. b. 1784	Quintet (Fl., Cl., Bn., Hn., Pno.)	Breitkopf; Doblinger
Szeligowski, T. b. 1896	Quintet	P.W.M., Warsaw
Taffanel, C. P. b. 1844	Quintet	Leduc
Telemann, G. P. b. 1681	Overture Suite (2 Obs., 2 Hns., Bn.)	Leuckart
Thomson, V. b. 1896	Sonata da Chiesa (E flat Cl., Hn., Tpt., Tromb., Va.)	New Music, N.Y.

CHAMBER MUSIC (*cont.*)

Tomasi, H. b. 1901	Variations sur un Thème Corse	Leduc
Van Praag, H. b. 1880	2 Quintets	Donemus
Valen, F. b. 1887	Serenade	Hinrichsen
Verall, J. b. 1908	Serenade	Mercury
Villa-Lobos, H. b. 1887	*Quintet (Fl., Ob., Cl., EH (or Hn.), Bn.)	Schott
Weis, F. b. 1898	Serenade	Hansen
Wellesz, E. b. 1885	Suite	U.E.
Zafred, M. b. 1922	Sinfonietta for WW. Quintet	Ricordi
Zender, H. b. 1936	Quintet	Peters

3) SIX TO NINE INSTRUMENTS

Addison, J. b. 1920	Serenade (WW. Quint, Hp)	O.U.P.
Angerer, P. b. 1927	Quinta Tön (WW. Quint., 2 Tpts., Tromb.)	U.E.
Baaren, K. v. b. 1906	*Septet (WW. Quint., Vn., Db.)	Donemus
Beethoven, L. v. b. 1772	Sextet (2 Cls., 2 Bns., 2 Hns.) Sextet (2 Hns., Str. Quart.) Septet (Cl., Bn., Hn., Str. Trio, Db.) Octet (2 Obs., 2 Cls., 2 Bns., 2 Hns.) Rondino (2 Obs., 2 Cls., 2 Bns., 2 Hns.)	
Berezowsky, N. b. 1900	Brass Suite (2 Tpts., 2 Hns., 2 Tromb., Tuba)	Mills
Berkeley, L. b. 1903	Sextet (Cl., Hn., Str. Quart.)	Chester
Boccherini, L. b. 1743	Sextet (Hn., 2 Vns., Va., 2 Vcs.)	Sikorski
Borkovec, P. b. 1894	*Nonet (WW. Quint., Str. Trio, Db.)	Hudebni

CHAMBER MUSIC (*cont.*)

Burkhard, W.
  b. 1900
	Serenade (Fl., Cl., Bn., Hn.,
	  Vn., Va., Db., Hp.)
		B. & H.

Chou,
  Wen-Chung
  b. 1923
	*Suite (WW. Quint., Hp.)	Peters

Clementi, A.
  b. 1925
	*Concertino (Fl., Ob., Bn., C.
	  Bn., Hn., Vn., Vc., Db.,
	  Pno)
		Zerboni

Crawford-
  Seeger, R.
  b. 1901
	*Suite (WW. Quint., Pno.)	MS.

Davies, P. M.
  b. 1934
	*Alma Redemptoris Mater (Fl.,
	  Ob., 2 Cls., Bn., Hn.)
		Schott

	*Ricercar and Doubles (WW. Quint., Va., Vc., Cemb.)	Schott
Dohnanyi, E. b. 1877	Sextet (Cl., Hn., Str. Trio, Pno.)	Lengnick-Mills
Dresden, S. b. 1881	3 Sextets (WW. Quint., Pno.)	Donemus

Fellegara, V.
  b. 1927
	*Octet (WW. Quint., 2 Tpt.,
	  Tromb.)
		Zerboni

Ferguson, H. b. 1908	Octet (Cl., Bn., Hn., Str. Quint.)	B. & H.

Flothuis, M.
  b. 1914
	Divertimento (Cl., Bn., Hn.,
	  Vn., Va., Db.)
		Donemus

Foerster, J. B.
  b. 1859
	*Nonet (WW. Quint., Str. Trio,
	  Db.)
		Hudebni

Fricker, P. R.
  b. 1920
	Octet (Fl., Cl., Bn., Hn., Str.
	  Trio, Db.)
		Schott

	3 Sonnets (Tenor, WW. Quint., Vc., Db.)	Schott

Gal, H.
  b. 1890
	Divertimento (Fl., Ob., 2 Cls.,
	  2 Hns., Bn., Tpt.)
		Leuckart

Gavazzeni, G.
  b. 1909
	Aria (Cl., 2 Hns., Str. Quint.)	Bongiovanni,
		  Bologna

Genzmer, H.
  b. 1909
	Septet (Fl., Cl., Hn., Str. Trio,
	  Hp.)
		Schott

Ghedini, G. F.
  b. 1892
	Adagio and Allegro (Fl., Cl.,
	  Hn., Str. Trio)
		Ricordi

Gilse, J. v.
  b. 1880
	Nonet (Ob., Cl., Bn., Hn., Str.
	  Quint.)
		Donemus

Goossens, E.
  b. 1893
	Fantasy Nonet (Fl., Ob., 2 Cls.,
	  2 Hns., 2 Bns., Tpt.)
		Curwen

CAHMBER MUSIC (*cont.*)

Gounod, Ch. b. 1818	Petite Symphonie (Fl., Ob., 2 Cls., 2 Bns., 2 Hns.)	Costallat
Gruenberg, L. b. 1882	The Creation (Tenor, Fl., Cl., Bn., Hn., Tpt., Perc., Pno., Va.)	U.E.
Haba, A. b. 1893	Septet (Cl., Bn., Hn., Str. Trio, Pno.)	Hudebni
	*Nonet (WW. Quint., Str. Trio, Db.)	Hudebni
Harsanyi, T. b. 1898	Nonet (WW. Quint., Str. Quart.)	Eschig
Haydn, J. b. 1732	Sextet (Ob., Bn., Hn., Str. Trio)	Musica Rara, London
	Octet (2 Obs., 2 Cls., 2 Hns., 2 Bns.)	Kahnt; Peters
Hill, E. B. b. 1872	Sextet (WW. Quint., Pno.)	Schirmer
Hindemith, P. b. 1895	Septet (WW. Quint., Bs. Cl., Tpt.)	Schott
	Octet (Cl., Bn., Hn., Str. Quint.)	Schott
Holbrooke, J. b. 1878	Sextet (WW. Quint., Pno.)	Chester
Hummel, J. N. b. 1778	Septet (Fl., Ob., Hn., Va., Vc., Db., Pno.)	Peters; Schott
Indy, V. d' b. 1851	Chansons et Danses (Fl., Ob., 2 Cls., Hn., 2 Bns.)	Durand
Ireland, J. b. 1879	Sextet (Cl., Hn., Str. Quart.)	
Janacek, L. b. 1854	*Sextet, Mladi (WW. Quint., Bs. Cl.)	Hudebni
	*Concertino (Cl., Bn., Hn., 2 Vns., Va., Pno.)	Hudebni
Johnson, J. J. b. 1924	*Turnpike (Cl., Fl., Ten. Sax., Bn., Hn., Tromb., Hp., Db., Dr.)	MJQ Music, N.Y.
Juon, P. b. 1872	Divertimento (WW. Quint., Pno.)	Lienau
Kahn, E. I. b. 1905	*Actus Tragicus (WW. Quint., Str. Quart.)	Bomart, N.Y.
Koechlin, Ch. b. 1867	Septet (WW. Quint, EH, Sax.)	L'Oiseau Lyre, Paris

CHAMBER MUSIC (*cont.*)

Kornauth, E. b. 1891	Nonet (Fl., Ob., Cl., Hn., Str. Quint.)	U.E.
Kreutzer, C. b. 1780	Septet (Cl., Bn., Hn., Str. Trio, Db.)	Chester
Kupferman, M. b. 1926	*Chamber Symphony (WW. Quint., Bs. Cl., Vn., Db.)	*MS.*
Leibowitz, R. b. 1913	Chamber Concerto (WW. Quint., Str. Trio., Db.)	U.E.
Lekeu, G. b. 1870	*Fantaisie Contrapuntique (Ob., Cl., Bn., Hn., Str. Quint.)	Salabert
Lewis, J. b. 1920	*Django (Fl., Cl., Ten. Sax., Bn., Hn., Tromb., Hp., Db., Dr.)	MJQ Music, N.Y.
	*The Queen's Fancy (Fl., Cl., Ten. Sax., Bn., Hn., Tromb., Hp., Db., Dr.)	MJQ Music, N.Y.
	*Exposure (Fl., Cl., Bn., Hn., Vib., Hp., Pno., Vc., Db., Dr.)	MJQ Music, N.Y.
Luening, O. b. 1900	Sextet (Fl., Cl., Hn., Str. Trio)	A.C.A., N.Y.
Malipiero, G. F. b. 1882	4 Old Songs (Voice, WW. Quint., Va., Db.)	Zerboni
	Ricercare; Ritrovare (WW. Quint., 4 Vas., Vc., Db.)	U.E.
Merikanto, A. b. 1893	Concerto (Vn., Cl., Hn., Str. Sextet)	Schott
Moscheles, I. b. 1794	Septet (Cl., Hn., Str. Trio, Db., Pno.)	**Kistner
Moser, Fr. b. 1880	Sinfonie for 9 Solo Instruments	Doblinger
Mozart, W. A. b. 1756	6 Divertimenti (2 Obs., 2 Bns., 2 Hns.)	
	Serenades No. 11 and 12 (2 Obs., 2 Cls., 2 Bns., 2 Hns.)	
	Serenade No. 10 (2 Obs., 2 Cls., 2 Bsst. Hns., 4 Hns., 2 Bns., C. Bn.)	
	Musikalischer Spass (2 Hns., Str. Quart.)	
Müller- Zürich, P. b. 1898	Marienleben (Fl., Ob., Cl., Hn., Str. Quint.)	Schott

CHAMBER MUSIC (*cont.*)

Nono, L. b. 1924	*Polofonica, Monodia, Ritmica (Fl., Cl., Bs. Cl., Hn., Alt. Sax., Pno., Perc.)	Ars Viva-Schott
Novak, J. b. 1921	*Balletti for Nonet (WW. Quint., Str. Trio., Db.)	Hudebni
Onslow, G. b. 1784	Septet (WW. Quint., Db., Pno.)	**Kistner
	Nonet (WW. Quint., Str. Quart.)	**Kistner
Paccagnini, A. b. 1930	*Musica da Camera (Picc., Fl., Bs. Cl., Hn., Hp., Vib., Vn., Vc., Db.)	U.E.
Paz, J. C. b. 1901	Concierto No. 2 (Ob., 2 Hns., Tpt., Bn., Pno.)	*MS.*
	Octet (Fl., Ob., 2 Bns., 2 Hns. 2 Tpts.)	*MS.*
Petyrek, F. b. 1892	Divertimento (2 Fls., Ob., Cl., 2 Bns., 2 Hns.)	U.E.
Pierné, G. b. 1863	Pastorale (Fl., Ob., Cl., Hn., 2 Bns., Tpt.)	Durand
Pijper, W. b. 1894	Sextet (WW. Quint., Pno.)	Donemus
	Septet (WW. Quint., Db., Pno.)	Donemus
Poulenc, F. b. 1899	Sextet (WW. Quint., Pno.)	Chester
Rebner, W. b. 1910	Sextet (WW. Quint., Bs. Cl.)	E.M.
Reinecke, K. b. 1824	Sextet (Fl., Ob., Cl., Bn., 2 Hns.)	**Kistner
	Octet (Fl., Ob., 2 Cls., 2 Bns., 2 Hns.)	**Zimmermann
Rheinberger, J. b. 1839	Nonet (WW. Quint., Str. Trio, Db.)	**Kistner
Ridky, J. b. 1897	*Nonet (WW. Quint., Str. Trio, Db.)	Hudebni
Riegger, W. b. 1885	*Concerto (WW. Quint., Pno.)	A.M.P., N.Y.
	*Nonet for Brass	A.M.P., N.Y.
Ries, F. b. 1784	Octet (Cl., Bn., Hn., Str. Trio, Db., Pno.)	**Kistner
Roussel, A. b. 1869	*Divertissement (WW. Quint., Pno.)	Rouart
Schat, P. b. 1935	*Septet (Fl., Ob., Cl., Hn., Vc., Pno., Perc.)	Donemus

CHAMBER MUSIC (*cont.*)

Schoeck, O. b. 1886	Serenade (WW. Quint., Str. Quart.)	Hug
Schubert, F. b. 1797	Octet (Cl., Bn., Hn., Str. Quint.)	
	Minuet and Finale (2 Obs., 2 Cls., 2 Bns., 2 Hns.)	Breitkopf
	Trauermusik (2 Cls., 2 Bns., 2 Hns., 2 Trombs., C. Bn.)	Breitkopf
Seiber, M. b. 1905	Serenade (2 Cls., 2 Bns., 2 Hns.)	Hansen
	Fantasy (Fl., Hn., Str. Quart.)	Zerboni
Shapey, R. b. 1921	*Concerto for Cl. and Chamber Group (Cl., Hn., Vn., Vc., Pno., Perc. (2 players))	Leeds, N.Y.
	*Incantations (Soprano, Alt. Sax., Hn., Tpt., Vc., Pno., Perc.(2 players))	Leeds, N.Y.
	*Dimensions (Soprano, Fl., Ob., [EH], Ten. Sax., Hn., Tpt., Pno., Db.)	Leeds, N.Y.
Smit, L. b. 1900	Sextet (WW., Quint., Pno.)	Donemus
Spohr, L. b. 1784	Nonet (Ob., Cl., Bn., Hn., Str. Quint.)	Peters
Starer, R. b. 1924	Suite for Brass	Mercury, N.Y.
Stöhr, R. b. 1874	Kammersinfonie (Ob., Cl., Bn., Hn., Hp., Str. Quart.)	**Kahnt
Stravinsky, I. b. 1882	*Septet (Cl., Bn., Hn., Str. Trio, Pno.)	B. & H.
Tansman, A. b. 1897	La Danse de la Sorcière (WW. Quint, Pno.)	Schott
Telemann, G. P. b. 1681	Suite (2 Hns., 2 Vns., Cont.)	Peters
Thuille, L. b. 1861	Sextet (WW. Quint., Pno.)	Breitkopf
Uhl, A. b. 1909	Octet (2 Obs., 2 Cls., 2 Bns., 2 Hns.)	U.E.
Varèse, E. b. 1885	*Octandre (WW. Quint., Tpt., Tromb., Db.)	Ricordi
Villa- Lobos, H. b. 1887	*Choros No. 3 (Cl., Alt. Sax., 3 Hns., Bn., Tromb., Men's Chorus)	Eschig

CHAMBER MUSIC (*cont.*)

Webern, A. b. 1883	*Two Songs, op. 8 (Mezzo Sop., Cl., Hn., Tpt., Hp., Cel., Str. Trio)	U.E.
	*Concerto for Nine Instruments (Fl., Ob., Cl., Hn., Tpt., Tromb., Vn., Va., Pno.)	U.E.
Weill, K. b. 1900	*Frauentanz (Sop., Fl., Cl., Bn., Hn., Va.)	U.E.
Wellesz, E. b. 1885	Octet (Cl., Bn., Hn., Str. Quint.)	Lengnick-Mills
Wyner, Y. b. 1929	*Serenade (Cl., Hn., Tpt., Tmb., Va., Vc., Pno.)	A.C.A., N.Y.
Yun, I. b. 1917	*Music for 7 Instruments (WW. Quint., Vn., Vc.)	Bote & Bock
Zagwijn, H. b. 1878	Nocturne (Fl., EH., Cl., Bn., Hn., Hp., Cel.)	Donemus
Zich, J. b. 1912	Octet (Hn., Bn., Str. Quint., Pno.)	Hudebni

4) TEN OR MORE INSTRUMENTS

Babbitt, M. b. 1916	Composition for Twelve Instruments (WW. Quint., Tpt., Hp., Cel., Str. Trio, Db.)	Bomart, N.Y
Berg, A. b. 1885	*Chamber Concerto (Solo Vn., Pno., Picc., Fl., Ob., EH, E flat Cl., Cl., Bs. Cl., Bn., C Bn., 2 Hns., Tpt., Tromb.)	U.E.
Berio, L. b. 1925	*Serenata for Solo Fl. and 14 Instr. (Solo Fl., Ob., EH., 2 Cls., Bn., Hn., Tpt., Tromb., Hp., Pno., Str. Trio, Db.)	Zerboni
Casadesus, R. b. 1899	Dixtuor (Dble. WW. Quint.)	Andraud, Cincinnati
Dvořák, A. b. 1841	*Serenade (Winds, Vc., Db.)	Bote & Bock
Enesco, G. b. 1881	Dixtuor (Dble. WW. Quint., EH. instead of 2nd Ob.)	**Enoch, Paris
Farkas, F. b. 1905	Kalender (Sop., Tenor, WW. Quint., Hp., Str. Quint.)	U.E.

CHAMBER MUSIC (*cont.*)

Giuffre, J. b. 1921	*Suspensions(Fl., Alt. Sax., Ten. Sax., Bn., Hn., Tpt., Tromb., Vib., Gtr., Pno., Db., Dr.)	MJQ Music, N.Y.
Goehr, A. b. 1932	*The Deluge (2 Voices, Fl., Tpt., Hn., Hp., Str. Trio, Db.)	Schott
Hindemith, P. b. 1895	*Kammermusik No. 2, Op. 36, No.1 (Solo Pno., WW. Quint. Bs. Cl., Tpt., Tromb., Str. Trio, Db.)	Schott
Kupferman, M. b. 1926	*Serial Variations for Chamber Orch. (Fl., Cl., 2 Hns., 2 Vns., 2 Vcs., Timp., Pno.)	*MS.*
Lampersberg, G. b. 1928	Musik for Oboe and 13 Instru- ments (Solo Ob., Bs. Cl., Bn., Hn., Tpt., Tromb., Hp., Pno., Cel., Perc., Str. Trio, Db.)	U.E.
Maderna, B. b. 1920	*Serenata (Fl., Cl., Bs. Cl., Hn., Tpt., Hp., Pno., Vn., Va., Db., Perc.)	Zerboni
Malipiero, G. b. 1882	Serenata Mattutina (Fl., Ob., Cl., 2 Bns., 2 Hns., Cel., 2 Vas.)	U.E.
Messiaen, O. b. 1908	Oiseaux Exotiques (Picc., Fl., Ob., E flat Cl. 2 Cls. Bs. Cl., Bn., 2 Hns., Tpt., 5 Perc., Solo Piano)	U.E.
Milhaud, D. b. 1892	*L'Homme et son Desir (Picc., Fl., Ob., EH., Cl., Bs. Cl., Bn., Hn., 2 Tpt., Perc., Hp., Str. Quint.)	U.E.
	*Dixtuor (Picc., Fl., Ob., EH., Cl., Bs. Cl., 2 Bns., 2 Hns.)	U.E.
	*Creation du Monde (2 Fls., Ob., 2 Cls., Bn., Hn., 2 Tpts., Tromb., Alt. Sax., Timp., Perc., 2 Vns., Vc., Ob., Pno.)	Eschig
Molbe, H. b. 1835	Dixtuor (Cl., EH., Bn., Hn., 3 Vns., Va., Vc., Db.)	Hofmeister
Mozart, W. A. b. 1756	2 Divertimenti (2 Obs., 2 EHs., 2 Cls., 2 Bns., 2 Hns.)	

CHAMBER MUSIC (*cont.*)

Paz., J. C. b. 1901	*Theme and Variations for 11 Instruments (Fl., Ob., 2 Cls., Bs. Cl., 2 Bns., 2 Hns., 2 Trombs.)	*MS.*
	*Overture for 12 Instruments (WW.Quint. plus extra Hn., Tpt., Tromb., Str. Trio, Db.)	
Perilhou, A. died 1936	Divertissement (Dble. WW. Quart., 4 Hns.)	Heugel
Poulenc, F. b. 1899	Mouvements Perpetuels (Fl., Ob., EH., Cl., Bn., Hn., Str. Quart.)	Chester
Pousseur, H. b. 1929	*Symphonies (WW. Quint., another Hn., Tpt., Tromb., 2 Hps., Pno., Str. Quint.)	U.E.
Reck, D. b. 1934	No. 1. (Fl., Cl., Ten. Sax., Hn., Gtr., Vib., Pno., 3 Perc.)	MJQ Music, N.Y.
Reicha, A. b. 1770	Dixtuor (WW. Quint., Str. Quint.)	**
Reizenstein, F. b. 1911	Serenade (Fl., 2 Obs., 2 Cls., 2 Bns., 2 Hns., Db.)	B. & H.
Rieti, V. b. 1898	Madrigal (WW. Quint., Tpt., Str. Quint., Pno.)	Salabert
Rosetti, A. b. 1750	*3 Parthias (various large en- sembles)	Breitkopf
Salmhofer, F. b. 1900	Kammersuite (Fl., Picc., 2 Obs., Cl., Bs. Cl., 2 Bns., 2 Hns., Hp., Str. Quint.)	U.E.
Schmitt, F. b. 1870	Lied et Scherzo (Solo Hn., 2 Fls., Ob., EH., 2 Cls., 2 Bns., Hn.)	Durand
Schönberg, A. b. 1874	*Kammersinfonie, op. 9 (Fl., Ob., EH., Cl. in D, Cl., Bs. Cl., Bn., C. Bn., 2 Hns., Str. Trio, Db.)	U.E.
	*Five Orchestral Pieces, op. 16 (transcr. for WW. Quint., Harmonium, Pno., Str. Quint.)	Litolff

CHAMBER MUSIC (*cont.*)

Schuller, G. b. 1925	Transformation (Fl., Cl., Ten. Sax, Bn., Hn., Tromb., Hp., Vib., Pno., Db., Dr.)	MJQ Music, N.Y.
	Symphony for Brass (6 Tpts., 4 Hns., 3 Trombs., Bari. Hn., 2 Tuba., Timp.)	Malcolm, N.Y.
Searle, H. b. 1915	Variations and Finale (WW. Quint., Str. Quint.)	Schott
Skalkottas, N. b. 1904	*Andante Sostenuto (Pno. Solo and 10 Wind Instruments.)	U.E.
Strauss, R. b. 1864	Suite, op. 4 (2 Fls., 2 Obs., 2 Cls., 3 Bns., 4 Hns.)	Leuckart
	Serenade, op. 7 (Dble. WW. Quart, C. Bn., 4 Hns.)	U.E.
	Symphony for Winds (Large ens., incl. 4 Hns.)	B. &. H.
Stravinsky, I. b. 1882	*Symphonies for Wind Instr. (Large ensemble, incl. 4 Hns.)	
	*Ragtime (Fl., Cl., Hn., Cornet, Tromb., 2 Vns., Va., Db., Cymbalum, Perc.)	Chester
Tomasi, H. b. 1901	Jeux de Geishas (WW. Quint., Str. Quint., Hp., Perc.)	Durand
Varèse, E. b. 1885	*Hyperprism (Fl., E flat Cl., 3 Hns., 2 Trombs., Perc.)	Ricordi
	*Intégrales (2 Piccs., E flat Cl., Cl., Ob., Hn., D Tpt., Tpt., 3 Trombs., 4 Percs.)	Ricordi